Essential HINDI

Speak Hindi With Confidence

Richard Delacy

TUTTLE Publishing

Tokyo | Rutland, Vermont | Singapore

The author would like to thank Mrs Sudha Joshi for proofreading the entire text. All inaccuracies remain the author's.

Published by Tuttle Publishing, an imprint of Periplus Editions (HK) Ltd.

www.tuttlepublishing.com

Library of Congress Control Number: 2014938779

ISBN 978-0-8048-4432-1

First edition
16 15 14   5 4 3 2 1   1406HP
Printed in Singapore

Distributed by
North America, Latin America & Europe
Tuttle Publishing
364 Innovation Drive
North Clarendon, VT 05759-9436 U.S.A.
Tel: 1 (802) 773-8930
Fax: 1 (802) 773-6993
info@tuttlepublishing.com
www.tuttlepublishing.com

Japan
Tuttle Publishing
Yaekari Building, 3rd Floor, 5-4-12 Osaki
Shinagawa-ku, Tokyo 141 0032
Tel: (81) 3 5437-0171
Fax: (81) 3 5437-0755
sales@tuttle.co.jp
www.tuttle.co.jp

Asia Pacific
Berkeley Books Pte. Ltd.
61 Tai Seng Avenue #02-12,
Singapore 534167
Tel: (65) 6280-1330
Fax: (65) 6280-6290
inquiries@periplus.com.sg
www.periplus.com

Contents

Introduction

● **Welcome to the Tuttle Essential Language series, covering all of the most popular world languages. These books are basic guides in communicating in the language. They're concise, accessible and easy to understand, and you'll find them indispensable on your trip abroad to get you where you want to go, pay the right prices and do everything you've been planning to do.**

This guide is divided into 16 themed sections and starts with a pronunciation table which explains the phonetic pronunciation to all the words and sentences you'll need to know, and a basic grammar guide which will help you construct basic sentences in your chosen language. At the end of the book is an extensive English–Hindi word list.

Throughout the book you'll come across boxes with a symbol beside them. These are designed to help you if you can't understand what your listener is saying to you. Hand the book over to them and encourage them to point to the appropriate answer to the question you are asking.

Other boxes in the book—this time without the symbol—give listings of themed words with their English translations.

For extra clarity, we have put all phonetic pronunciations of the foreign language terms in bold italic.

This book covers all subjects you are likely to come across during the course of a visit, from reserving a room for the night to ordering food and drink at a restaurant and what to do if your car breaks down or you lose your money. With over 2,000 commonly used words and essential sentences at your fingertips you can rest assured that you will be able to get by in all situations, so let **Essential Hindi** become your passport to learning to speak with confidence!

Pronunciation guide

The Hindi syllabary is made up of forty-six characters in their basic form. There are eleven vowels and thirty-six consonants. Ten of the eleven vowels also have an abbreviated form, when they are pronounced together with a consonant. Unless a consonant is written with one of the abbreviated forms of these ten vowels, it is either pronounced with an inherent a अ vowel, or, depending on its place in the word, with no vowel sound.

Guide to Pronunciation

Roman	Devanagari		Phonetic Description	Approximate Pronunciation
a	अ		mid-central unrounded vowel	***a*** as in sun
ā	आ	ा *	low-central unrounded vowel	***ā*** as in father
i	इ	ि *	high front unrounded vowel	***i*** as in sin
ī	ई	ी *	long high front vowel	***ī*** as in feed
u	उ	ु *	short high back rounded vowel	***u*** as in book
ū	ऊ	ू *	long high back rounded vowel	***ū*** as in food
ṛ	ऋ	ृ *	voiced alveolar trill + high front unrounded vowel	***ṛi*** as in ring
e	ए	े *	high mid-front rounded vowel	***e*** as in bet
ai	ऐ	ै *	long low front vowel and diphthong	***ai*** as in height
o	ओ	ो *	long rounded back mid vowel	***o*** as in so
au	औ	ौ *	low-mid to mid-back rounded vowel	***au*** as in how

* When written with a consonant, these symbols indicate that these vowel sounds are pronounced with the consonant in place of the inherent 'a' vowel. See the Rules for pronunciation below.

Roman	Devanagari	Phonetic Description	Approximate Pronunciation
ka	क	voiceless unaspirated velar plosive	***ka*** as in speaker
kha	ख	voiceless aspirated velar plosive	***kha*** as in blockhead
ga	ग	voiced unaspirated velar plosive	***ga*** as in gun
gha	घ	voiced aspirated velar plosive	***gha*** as in loghouse
ṅ	ङ	velar nasal plosive	***ṅa*** as in king
ca	च	voiceless unaspirated palatoalveolar affricative	***ca*** as in chutney
cha	छ	voiceless aspirated palatoalveolar affricative	***cha*** as in church-hill
ja	ज	voiced unaspirated palatoalveolar affricative	***ja*** as in judge
jha	झ	voiced aspirated palatoalveolar affricative	***jha*** as in hedgehog
ña	ञ	palatal nasal plosive	***ña*** as in crunch
ṭa	ट	voiceless unaspirated retroflex plosive	tongue touches the top of the mouth
ṭha	ठ	voiceless unaspirated retroflex plosive	tongue touches the top of the mouth, breath of air accompanies the sound
ḍa	ड	voiced unaspirated retroflex plosive	tongue touches the top of the mouth
ṛa	ड़	voiced unaspirated retroflex flap	tongue touches the top of the mouth and, without resting there, flaps down
ḍha	ढ	voiced aspirated retroflex plosive	tongue touches the top of the mouth; a breath of air accompanies the sound
ṛha	ढ़	voiced aspirated retroflex flap	tongue touches the top of the mouth and, without resting there, flaps down; a breath of air accompanies the sound

Roman	Devanagari	Phonetic Description	Approximate Pronunciation
ṇa	ण/ण	retroflex nasal plosive	tongue touches the top of the mouth
ta	त	voiceless unaspirated dental plosive	tongue touches the back of the top teeth
tha	थ	voiceless aspirated dental plosive	tongue touches the back of the top teeth; a breath of air accompanies the sound
da	द	voiced unaspirated dental plosive	tongue touches the back of the top teeth
dha	ध	voiced aspirated dental plosive	tongue touches the back of the top teeth; a breath of air accompanies the sound
na	न	voiced unaspirated dental nasal plosive	tongue touches the back of the top teeth
pa	प	voiceless unaspirated bilabial plosive	***pa*** as in s<u>p</u>un
pha	फ	voiced unaspirated bilabial plosive	***pha*** as in <u>p</u>utt
ba	ब	voiced unaspirated bilabial plosive	***ba*** as in <u>b</u>ut
bha	भ	aspirated bilabial plosive	***bha*** as in clu<u>bh</u>ouse
ma	म	bilabial nasal	***ma*** as in <u>m</u>oney
ya	य	voiced palatal semi-vowel	***ya*** as in <u>y</u>oung
ra	र	voiced alveolar trill	***ra*** as in <u>r</u>un
la	ल	voiced alveolar lateral	***la*** as in <u>l</u>ung
va/wa	व	voiced labio-dental semi-vowel or fricative	sometimes closer to a 'v' and sometimes to a 'w'
śa	श	voiceless prepalatal fricative	***śa*** as in <u>sh</u>un
ṣa	ष	voiceless retroflex sibilant fricative	***ṣa*** as in flu<u>sh</u>
sa	स	voiceless alveolar sibilant fricative	***sa*** as in <u>s</u>un
ha	ह	voiced or unvoiced fricative	***ha*** as in <u>h</u>unt

There are some sounds in Hindi that were originally not represented in the script. They occur in words that came into Hindi from Arabic, Persian and English, among other languages. They are represented by dots under particular characters.

Roman	Devanagari	Phonetic Description	Approximate Pronunciation
qa	क़	voiceless, unaspirated velar plosive	produced further back in the throat than '***ka***'
<u>kh</u>a	ख़	velar fricative	there is a partial closure of the air passage
<u>gh</u>a	ग़	post-velar fricative	produced like '***ga***' but further back in the thoat
za	ज़	voiced alveolar fricative	***za*** as in <u>z</u>ebra
fa	फ़	labio-dental fricative	***fa*** as in <u>f</u>un

Rules for pronunciation

1) Each consonant is pronounced with an inherent '***a***' अ vowel, except in the following circumstances:

a) an abbreviated vowel symbol is written with it

For example:

क = ***ka*** but

का = ***kā***; कि = ***ki***; की = ***kī***; कु = ***ku***; कू = ***kū***; कृ = ***kṛ***; के = ***ke***;
कै = ***kai***; को = ***ko***; कौ = ***kao***

b) at the end of a word

For example:

काम = ***kām***

c) it is not being omitted twice in a row

For example:

कमला = ***kamlā***; नमक = ***namak***

d) its form is modified and it is connected to the following consonant

For example:

क् ***k*** + य ***ya*** = क्य ***kya***

Most of these modified forms will be easily recognizable. Some, however, are a bit more idiosyncratic.

2) Occasionally when an ***a*** अ vowel is followed by an ***ha*** ह् with which no full vowel is pronounced, this ***a*** अ is pronounced as a short ***e*** ए.

For example:

महल = ***mehal*** (palace) (in this word the ***a*** vowel is very short)

Conjunct Consonants

Most modified forms of consonants joined together to indicate the omission of an intervening '***a***' vowel will be readily identifiable (such as क् ***k*** + य ***ya*** = क्य ***kya*** above). However, the constituent consonants in some clusters are not so recognizable. For a list of these, refer to a standard text like *Elementary Hindi*, pp. 42–46.

Basic grammar

The most important features of Hindi grammar are the conjugations of verbs, and the use of postpositions (the same as prepositions in English, except that they follow the word to which they relate).

One of the most important rules of Hindi grammar is that *any word that is followed by a postposition cannot influence the conjugation of the verb*. Sometimes postpositions in Hindi are implied (that is, not visible). Depending on the word that is being governed by a postposition, its form may have to change when it is followed by a postposition.

For example:

that ***voh*** वह

those ***vo*** वे

good ***acchā*** अच्छा

boy (m) ***laṛkā*** लड़का

that good boy ***voh acchā laṛkā*** वह अच्छा लड़का

to that good boy ***us acche laṛke KO*** उस अच्छे लड़के को

those good boys ***vo acche laṛke*** वे अच्छे लड़के

to those good boys ***un acche laṛkõ KO*** उन अच्छे लड़कों को

In the second and fourth examples above the postposition 'to' ***ko*** को appears. Look closely at the changes that have taken place to the words for 'that/those', 'good' and 'boy.' These changes tell us whether these words are singular or plural and followed by a postposition or not.

Word Order

Hindi is a subject-object-verb language (SOV).

For example:

I read a book. ***maĩ kitāb paṛhtā hū̃.*** मैं किताब पढ़ता हूँ।
S V O S O V

Nouns

All nouns in Hindi are either masculine or feminine. The form of many changes when they are pluralized and when followed by a postposition (*on, at, in, with,* etc). How they change depends on the ending of the word and its gender.

Nouns are declined according to the following rules.

Masculine Nouns

1. Masculine nouns that end in ***ā*** आ decline in the following manner.

Singular, – postposition	Singular, + postposition	Plural, – postposition	Plural, + postposition
kamrā कमरा room	***kamre mẽ*** कमरे में in a/the room	***kamre*** कमरे rooms	***kamrõ mẽ*** कमरों में in (the) rooms

2. All other masculine nouns decline in the following manner.

Singular, – postposition	Singular, + postposition	Plural, – postposition	Plural, + postposition
ghar घर home	***ghar mẽ*** घर में in a/the home	***ghar*** घर homes	***gharõ mẽ*** घरों में in (the) homes

Masculine nouns that end in the long vowels ***ī*** ई and ***ū*** ऊ shorten these vowels in the plural form with a postposition, and in the case of ***ī*** ई, add the semi-vowel ***y*** य् before the ending ***õ*** ओं.

Singular, – postposition	Singular, + postposition	Plural, – postposition	Plural, + postposition
ādmī आदमी a/the man	***ādmī mẽ*** आदमी में in a/the man	***ādmī*** आदमी men	***ādmiyõ mẽ*** आदमियों में in (the) men
ālū आलू potato	***ālū mẽ*** आलू में in a/the potato	***ālū*** आलू potatoes	***āluõ mẽ*** आलुओं में in (the) potatoes

3. There are some ***ā*** आ ending masculine nouns that follow the pattern of (2). These are mainly nouns that signify a relationship and have a reduplicative form as well as some words from Sanskrit. For example:

   maternal uncle ***māmā*** मामा

   paternal uncle ***cācā*** चाचा

   maternal grandfather ***nānā*** नाना

   paternal grandfather ***dādā*** दादा

   king ***rājā*** राजा

   father ***pitā*** पिता

Singular, – postposition	Singular, + postposition	Plural, – postposition	Plural, + postposition
rājā राजा a/the king	***rājā mẽ*** राजा में in a/the king	***rājā*** राजा kings	***rājāõ mẽ*** राजाओं में in (the) kings
māmā मामा maternal uncle	***māmā mẽ*** मामा में in an/the uncle	***māmā*** मामा uncles	***māmāõ mẽ*** मामाओं में in (the) uncles

Feminine Nouns

1. Feminine nouns that end in ***i*** इ, ***ī*** ई or ***iyā*** इया

   i इ — add ***yā̃*** याँ in plural with no postposition, ***yõ*** यों in plural with a postposition.

   ī ई — shorten to ***i*** इ and add ***yā̃*** याँ in plural with no postposition, ***yõ*** यों in plural with a postposition.

iyā इया — add ~ ँ in plural with no postposition, changing ***yā*** या to ***yõ*** यों in plural with a postposition.

Singular, – postposition	**Singular, + postposition**	**Plural, – postposition**	**Plural, + postposition**
rātri रात्रि night	***rātri mẽ*** रात्रि में in a/the night	***rātriyā̃*** रात्रियाँ nights	***rātriyõ mẽ*** रात्रियों में in (the) nights
sāṛī साड़ी sari	***sāṛī mẽ*** साड़ी में in a/the sari	***sāṛiyā̃*** साड़ियाँ saris	***sāṛiyõ mẽ*** साड़ियों में in (the) saris
ciṛiyā चिड़िया bird	***ciṛiyā mẽ*** चिड़िया में in a/the bird	***ciṛiyā̃*** चिड़ियाँ birds	***ciṛiyõ mẽ*** चिड़ियों में in (the) birds

2. Feminine nouns ending in any other character are declined simply by adding ***ẽ*** एँ in the plural form without a postposition, and ***õ*** ओं in the plural with a postposition.

Singular, – postposition	**Singular, + postposition**	**Plural, – postposition**	**Plural, + postposition**
cīz चीज़ thing	***cīz mẽ*** चीज़ में in a/the thing	***cīzẽ*** चीज़ें things	***cīzõ mẽ*** चीज़ों में in (the) things
bhāṣā भाषा language	***bhāṣā mẽ*** भाषा में in a/the language	***bhāṣāẽ*** भाषाएँ languages	***bhāṣāõ mẽ*** भाषाओं में in (the) languages
jorū जोरू wife	***jorū mẽ*** जोरू में in a/the wife	***jorūẽ*** जोरुएँ* wives	***jorūõ mẽ*** जोरुओं* में in (the) wives

* Feminine words ending in a ***ū*** ऊ vowel shorten this vowel before the addition of ***ẽ*** एँ and ***õ*** ओं in the plural with and without a postposition.

Adjectives

Adjectives in Hindi must also be declined according to their endings.

1. ***ā*** आ ending adjectives must change for the number, gender and case (occurrence of a postposition) of the noun that follows.

   good (adj) ***acchā*** अच्छा

good boy ***acchā laṛkā*** अच्छा लड़का	good girl ***acchī laṛkī*** अच्छी लड़की
good boys ***acche laṛke*** अच्छे लड़के	good girls ***acchī laṛkiyā̃*** अच्छी लड़कियाँ
to the good boy ***acche laṛke ko*** अच्छे लड़के को	to the good girl ***acchī laṛkī ko*** अच्छी लड़की को
to the good boys ***acche laṛkõ ko*** अच्छे लड़कों को	to the good girls ***acchī laṛkiyõ ko*** अच्छी लड़कियों को

2. Adjectives that end in any other character do not change.

   red (adj) ***lāl*** लाल

   red book (f) ***lāl kitāb*** लाल किताब

   red books (f, pl) ***lāl kitābẽ*** लाल किताबें

   in the red book (f) ***lāl kitāb mẽ*** लाल किताब में

   in the red books (f, pl) ***lāl kitābõ mẽ*** लाल किताबों में

There are some ***ā*** आ ending adjectives that do not change, and a few where it is up to the speaker's discretion. Here is a list of a few of the more common ones.

one-and-a-quarter ***savā*** सवा

excellent ***baṛhiyā*** बढ़िया

inferior ***ghaṭiyā*** घटिया

unfortunate, unhappy, sad ***dukhiyā*** दुखिया

born ***paidā*** पैदा

a little ***zarā*** ज़रा

alive ***zindā*** ज़िंदा

fresh ***tāzā*** ताज़ा (This may change according to the speaker's discretion.)

Pronouns

The forms of pronouns also change when they are followed by postpositions. Here is a list of all of possible forms of the pronouns with different postpositions. Postpositions can be made up of a single word (in ***mẽ*** में) or two or more words (for the sake of ***ke liye*** के लिये). In some cases, there are variant forms of some of the pronouns with particular postpositions.

Pronoun, – Post-position	**Pronoun, + Postposition**				
	+ ***kā*** + का 's	+ ***ke liye*** + के लिये for, in order to	+ ***mẽ*** + में in	+ ***ko*** + को (object marker)	+ ***ne*** + ने (ergative part)
I ***mẽ*** मैं	***merā*** मेरा	***mere liye*** मेरे लिये	***mujh mẽ*** मुझमें	***mujh ko/ mujhe*** मुझको/मुझे	***maĩ ne*** मैंने
we ***ham*** हम	***hamārā*** हमारा	***hamāre liye*** हमारे लिये	***ham mẽ*** हममें	***ham ko/ hamẽ*** हमको/हमें	***ham ne*** हमने
you ***tū*** तू	***terā*** तेरा	***tere liye*** तेरे लिये	***tujh mẽ*** तुझमें	***tujh ko/ tujhe*** तुझको/तुझे	***tū ne*** तूने
you ***tum*** तुम	***tumhārā*** तुम्हारा	***tumhāre liye*** तुम्हारे लिये	***tum mẽ*** तुममें	***tum ko/ tumhẽ*** तुमको/तुम्हें	***tum ne*** तुमने
you ***āp*** आप	***āp kā*** आपका	***āpke liye*** आपके लिये	***āp mẽ*** आपमें	***āp ko*** आपको	***āp ne*** आपने

Pronoun, – Post-position	Pronoun, + Postposition				
he/she/it/ this ***yeh*** यह	***is kā*** इसका	***is ke liye*** इसके लिये	***is mẽ*** इसमें	***is ko/ise*** इसको/इसे	***is ne*** इसने
he/she/it/ that ***voh*** वह	***us kā*** उसका	***us ke liye*** उसके लिये	***us mẽ*** उसमें	***us ko/use*** उसको/उसे	***us ne*** उसने
he/she/ they/ these ***ye*** ये	***in kā*** इनका	***in ke liye*** इनके लिये	***in mẽ*** इनमें	***in ko/inhẽ*** इनको/इन्हें	***inhõ ne*** इन्होंने
he/she/ they/those ***vo*** वे	***un kā*** उनका	***un ke liye*** उनके लिये	***un mẽ*** उनमें	***un ko/unhẽ*** उनको/उन्हें	***unhõ ne*** उन्होंने
who ***kaun*** कौन	***kis kā*** किसका	***kis ke liye*** किसके लिये	***kis mẽ*** किसमें	***kis ko/kise*** किसको/ किसे	***kis ne*** किसने
who (pl) ***kaun*** कौन	***kin kā*** किनका	***kin ke liye*** किनके लिये	***kin mẽ*** किनमें	***kin ko/ kinhẽ*** किनको/ किन्हें	***kinhõ ne*** किन्होंने
what ***kyā*** क्या	***kis kā*** किसका	***kis ke liye*** किसके लिये	***kis mẽ*** किसमें	***kis ko/kise*** किसको/ किसे	***kis ne*** किसने
someone/ anyone some/any ***koī*** कोई	***kisī kā*** किसी का	***kisī ke liye*** किसी के लिये	***kisī mẽ*** किसी में	***kisī ko*** किसी को	***kisī ne*** किसी ने
some (pl) ***koī*** कोई	***kinhī̃ kā*** किन्हीं का	***kinhī̃ ke liye*** किन्हीं के लिये	***kinhī̃ mẽ*** किन्हीं में	***kinhī̃ ko*** किन्हीं को	***kinhī̃ ne*** किन्हीं ने
who/that/ which ***jo*** जो	***jis kā*** जिसका	***jis ke liye*** जिसके लिये	***jis mẽ*** जिसमें	***jis ko/jise*** जिसको/ जिसे	***jis ne*** जिसने
who/that/ which (pl) ***jo*** जो	***jin kā*** जिनका	***jin ke liye*** जिनके लिये	***jin mẽ*** जिनमें	***jin ko/jinhẽ*** जिनको/ जिन्हें	***jinhõ ne*** जिन्होंने

Many of these postpositions are written together with pronouns in the Devanagari script. They have been written separately in the Roman script to show clearly the form that the pronoun takes.

Plural forms of pronouns are used for single people to be polite.

There are three second person pronouns. They function in the following manner:

you ***tū*** (sing) तू (intimate): used with animals, small children, god, intimate relations

you ***tum*** (pl) तुम (familiar): used with friends, family, people of same social standing

you ***āp*** आप (pl) (polite): used for respect with elders and people of higher social standing

There are only a few single word postpositions. They are:

's ***kā*** का

to (object marker) ***ko*** को

until, by ***tak*** तक

on, at, in ***par*** पर

in ***mẽ*** में

from, by, since, with ***se*** से

ergative particle ***ne*** ने

The majority of postpositions contain more than one word. Most are made up of two words, the first of which is either ***ke*** के or ***kī*** की.

with ***ke sāth*** के साथ

for (the sake of) ***ke liye*** के लिये

about, concerning ***ke bāre mẽ*** के बारे में; because of ***kī vajah se*** की वजह से

Verbs

Verbs are conjugated in the various tenses for the number, gender, and person of the subject. The verbal system is based on two participles:

the imperfect participle (action 'imperfect', or incomplete)

the perfect participle (action 'perfect', or complete)

These participles are effectively ***ā*** आ ending adjectives. (See above how adjectives function.) They are formed in the following manner:

- Imperfect participle: stem of a verb + ***tā/te/tī*** + ता/ते/ती

For example:

to speak

bolnā (infinitive)	***bol*** (stem) + ***tā/te/tī***	speak ***boltā/bolte/boltī***
बोलना	बोल + ता/ते/ती	बोलता/बोलते/बोलती

- Perfect participle: stem of a verb + ***ā/e/ī/ī̃*** + आ/ए/ई/ईं

For example:

to speak

bolnā (infinitive)	***bol*** (stem) + ***ā/e/ī/ī̃***	spoke ***bolā/bole/bolī/bolī̃***
बोलना	बोल + आ/ए/ई/ईं	बोला/बोले/बोली/बोलीं

These participles are then combined with the forms of the verb *to be* in the simple present and past.

Simple Present of the Verb *to be*

	Singular	**Plural**
1st person	I am ***maĩ hū̃*** मैं हूँ	we are ***ham haĩ*** हम हैं
2nd person	you are ***tū hai*** तू है	you are ***tum ho*** तुम हो
		you are ***āp haĩ*** आप हैं
3rd person	he/she/it/this is ***yeh hai*** यह है	these/they are ***ye haĩ*** ये हैं
	he/she/it/that is ***voh hai*** वह है	those/they are ***vo haĩ*** वे हैं

Simple Past of the Verb *to be*

	Singular (m/f)	Plural (m/f)
1st person	I am ***maĩ thā/thī*** मैं था/थी	we were ***ham the/thī̃*** हम थे/थीं
2nd person	you were ***tū thā/thī*** तू था/थी	you were ***tum the/thī̃*** तुम थे/थीं
		you were ***āp the/thī̃*** आप थे/थीं
3rd person	he/she/it/this was ***yeh thā/thī*** यह था/थी	these/they were (he/she was) ***ye the/thī̃*** ये थे/थीं
	he/she/it/that was ***voh thā/thī*** वह था/थी	those/they were (he/she was) ***vo the/thī̃*** वे थे/थीं

The two participles with these forms of the verb *to be* combine to form five of the six tenses.

I (m) speak ***maĩ boltā hū̃*** मैं बोलता हूँ (imperfect present)

I (m) used to speak ***maĩ boltā thā*** मैं बोलता था (habitual past)

I (m) spoke ***maĩ bolā*** मैं बोला (past)

I (m) have spoken ***maĩ bolā hū̃*** मैं बोला हूँ (present perfect)

I (m) had spoken ***maĩ bolā thā*** मैं बोला था (past perfect)

I (f) speak ***maĩ boltī hū̃*** मैं बोलती हूँ (imperfect present)

I (f) used to speak ***maĩ boltī thī*** मैं बोलती थी (habitual past)

I (f) spoke ***maĩ bolī*** मैं बोली (past)

I (f) have spoken ***maĩ bolī hū̃*** मैं बोली हूँ (present perfect)

I (f) had spoken ***maĩ bolī thī*** मैं बोली थी (past perfect)

Optative and Future Tense

The optative form of the verb expresses wishes, desires, possibilities, etc., and the future tense expresses actions that take place in the future.

Singular	Plural
I may/should speak ***maĩ bolũ*** मैं बोलूँ	we may/should speak ***ham bolẽ*** हम बोलें
you may/should speak ***tū bole*** तू बोले	you may/should speak ***tum bolo*** तुम बोलो you may/should speak ***āp bolẽ*** आप बोलें
he/she/it/this may/should speak ***yeh bole*** यह बोले	they/these/he/she may/should speak ***ye bolẽ*** ये बोलें
he/she/it/that may/should speak ***voh bole*** वह बोले	they/those/he/she may/should speak ***vo bolẽ*** वे बोलें

The future tense is formed by adding the ending ***gā/ge/gī*** गा/गे/गी to these forms.

For example:

I (m) will speak ***maĩ bolũgā*** मैं बोलूँगा

You (m, pl) will speak ***āp bolẽge*** आप बोलेंगे

He (m) will speak ***yeh bolegā*** यह बोलेगा

I (f) will speak ***maĩ bolũgī*** मैं बोलूँगी

You (f, pl) will speak ***āp bolẽgī*** आप बोलेंगी

She (f) will speak ***yeh bolegī*** यह बोलेगी

The Progressive Aspect

Actions can also be expressed as taking place at a particular moment, either in the present (or near future), or in the past.

This is formed in the following manner.

stem + ***rahā/rahe/rahī*** + tense marker

बोल (speaking) + रहा/रहे/रही + verb *to be* (present or past)

he is speaking ***voh bol rahā hai*** वह बोल रहा है

she is speaking ***voh bol rahī hai*** वह बोल रही है

he was speaking ***voh bol rahā thā*** वह बोल रहा था

she was speaking ***voh bol rahī thī*** वह बोल रही थी

they (m) are speaking ***vo bol rahe haĩ*** वे बोल रहे हैं

they (f) were speaking ***vo bol rahī thī̃*** वे बोल रही थीं

Imperatives

Commands are given to the second person (you). There are five forms of the imperative. These correspond to the three forms of the second person pronoun, and indicate the degree of respect (initimate, informal, polite, neutral/future, polite future).

You speak! ***tū bol!*** तू बोल! (stem of the verb 'to speak' ***bolnā*** बोलना, ***bol*** बोल) (intimate, impolite form)

You speak. ***tum bolo.*** तुम बोलो। (stem + ***o*** ओ) (familiar form)

You please speak. ***āp boliye.*** आप बोलिये। (stem + ***iye*** इये) (polite form)

You speak. (further in the future than now) ***tū/tum bolnā.*** तू/तुम बोलना। (infinitive of the verb) (neutral)

You please speak. (further in the future than now) ***āp boliyegā.*** आप बोलियेगा। (stem + ***iyegā*** इयेगा) (polite)

Sometimes the word ***zarā*** ज़रा 'a little' is used to soften an imperative.

Imperatives are negated using either

mat मत (more informal) or ***na*** न (more formal)

The following verbs have irregular forms when used with the familiar second person pronoun ***tum*** तुम:

to give ***denā*** देना – ***do*** दो

to take ***lenā*** लेना – ***lo*** लो

The following verbs have irregular forms when used with the polite second person pronoun ***āp*** आप:

to give ***denā*** देना – ***dījiye*** दीजिये

to take ***lenā*** लेना – ***lījiye*** लीजिये

to do ***karnā*** करना – ***kījiye*** कीजिये

to drink ***pīnā*** पीना – ***pījiye*** पीजिये

Asking Questions

Most question words appear directly before the verb. Question words begin with the character ***k*** क्

who ***kaun*** कौन	how ***kaisā/kaise*** कैसा/कैसे
when ***kab*** कब	why ***kyõ*** क्यों
where ***kahā̃*** कहाँ	what ***kyā*** क्या

For example:

Who was he? ***voh kaun thā?*** वह कौन था?

The word ***kyā*** क्या also appears at the beginning of a sentence, where it simply marks a question.

He is a good boy. ***voh acchā laṛkā hai.*** वह अच्छा लड़का है।

Is he a good boy? ***kyā voh acchā laṛkā hai?*** क्या वह अच्छा लड़का है?

The Use of ne ने

The postposition ***ne*** ने marks the subject of a transitive verb in the perfective form. If an object is expressed and unmarked by a postposition, the verb is conjugated for gender and number of it. If no object is expressed, the verb occurs in the masculine, singular form.

He (m) reads a book (f).	***voh kitāb paṛhtā hai.***	वह किताब पढ़ता है।
He (m) read a book (f).	***usne kitāb paṛhī.***	उसने किताब पढ़ी।
She (f) saw a boy (m).	***usne laṛke ko dekhā.***	उसने लड़के को देखा।

An Important Note

In this book, often you will see two forms of the same word separated by a '/' and then '(m/f)'. This indicates that the first form is the masculine form (either singular or plural), and the second is the feminine form.

For example:

How are you? (m/f)	***āp kaise/kaisī haĩ?*** आप कैसे/कैसी हैं?

1 The Basics

1. The Basics

1.1 Personal details

family name (m)	***parivār kā nām*** परिवार का नाम
name (m)	***nām*** नाम
address (m)	***patā*** पता
sex (male/female) (m)	***liṅg (puruṣ/strī)*** लिंग (पुरुष/स्त्री)
nationality (f)	***nāgriktā*** नागरिकता
date of birth (f)	***janmtithi*** जन्मतिथि
place of birth (m)	***janmsthān*** जन्मस्थान
occupation (m)	***peśā*** पेशा
married/unmarried	***vivāhit/avivāhit*** विवाहित/अविवाहित
children (m, pl)	***bāl bacce*** बाल बच्चे
place (m) and date (f) of issue	***jārī karne kā sthān aur tārīkh*** जारी करने का स्थान और तारीख़
passport/license number (m)	***pārpatra/lāisens kā nambar*** पारपत्र/लाइसेंस का नम्बर
signature (m, pl)	***hastākṣar*** हस्ताक्षर

1.2 Today or tomorrow?

What (which) day is it today?	***āj kaun-sā din hai?*** आज कौन-सा दिन है?	
Today is Monday. (the day of the moon)	***āj somvār (m) hai.*** आज सोमवार है।	
Tuesday (the day of Mars)	***maṅgal(vār) (m)*** मंगल(वार)	
Wednesday (the day of Mercury)	***budh(vār) (m)*** बुध(वार)	
Thursday (the day of Jupiter)	***guru(vār) (m)*** गुरु(वार)	***bṛhaspativār (m)*** बृहस्पतिवार
Friday (the day of Venus)	***śukra(vār) (m)*** शुक्र(वार)	
Saturday (the day of Saturn)	***śani(vār) (m)*** शनिवार	***śaniścar (m)*** शनिश्चर
Sunday (the day of the Sun)	***ravi(vār) (m)*** रविवार	***itvār (m)*** इतवार

Where the word वार ***vār*** (day) appears in parantheses, it may be omitted in spoken language. There are alternative words for Thursday, Saturday and Sunday.

When time words are used adverbially (*on* Monday, *in* the morning, *at* four o'clock) in Hindi, they are considered to be in the oblique case. This means that they are often, but not always, followed by a *postposition* (the same as a preposition in English, except that it follows the word), and often, but not always, their form changes. For more on the oblique case, see page 11. In the roman script, the postposition is place in capital letters to draw attention to its use.

We (m) will come on Monday.	***ham somvār KO āẽge.*** हम सोमवार को आएँगे।	
in the morning	***savere (m)/subah (f)*** सवेरे/सुबह	***saverā (m)*** सवेरा (morning)

during the day	***din (m) MẼ*** दिन में
in the afternoon/ at midday	***dopahar (f) KO*** दोपहर को
in the evening	***śām (f) KO*** शाम को
at night	***rāt (f) KO*** रात को
during the night	***rāt (f) MẼ*** रात में
today	***āj*** आज
tomorrow/yesterday	***kal (ko)*** कल (को)
the day after tomorrow/ before yesterday	***parsõ*** परसों
this morning	***āj savere/subah*** आज सवेरे/सुबह
this evening	***āj śām KO*** आज शाम को
tonight	***āj rāt KO*** आज रात को
on Tuesday morning	***maṅgal ko savere/subah*** मंगल को सवेरे/सुबह
on Tuesday evening	***maṅgal kī śām KO*** मंगल की शाम को
on that day	***us din*** उस दिन
(on) those days	***un dinõ*** उन दिनों
these days	***ājkal*** आजकल

in January	***janvarī MẼ*** जनवरी में
since (from) January	***janvarī SE*** जनवरी से

Months of the Year

The Hindi versions of the Gregorian calendar months are the most commonly employed names for the months of the year.

Gregorian Month		Hindi Name	Sanskrit Name
January (f)	***janvarī*** जनवरी	***māgh*** माघ	***māgh*** माघ
February (f)	***farvarī*** फ़रवरी	***phāgun*** फागुन	***phālgun*** फाल्गुन
March (m)	***mārc*** मार्च	***cait*** चैत	***caitra*** चैत्र
April (m)	***aprail*** अप्रैल	***baisākh*** बैसाख	***vaiśākh*** वैशाख
May (f)	***maī*** मई	***jeṭh*** जेठ	***jyeṣṭh*** ज्येष्ठ
June (m)	***jūn*** जून	***asāṛh*** असाढ़	***āṣāḍh*** आषाढ
July (f)	***julāī*** जुलाई	***sāvan*** सावन	***śrāvaṇ*** श्रावण
August (m)	***agast*** अगस्त	***bhādõ*** भादों	***bhādrapad*** भाद्रपद
September (m)	***sitambar*** सितम्बर	***kvār*** क्वार	***āśvin*** आश्विन
October (m)	***aktūbar*** अक्तूबर	***kārttik*** कार्त्तिक	***kārtik*** कार्तिक
November (m)	***navambar*** नवम्बर	***aghan*** अगहन	***agrahāyaṇ*** अग्रहायण

December (m)	***disambar*** दिसंबर	***pūs*** पूस	***pauṣ*** पौष

in summer ([in] the days of heat)	***garmī ke dinõ (MẼ)**** गर्मी के दिनों (में)
in winter ([in] the days of cold)	***ṭhaṇḍ ke dinõ (MẼ)**** ठंड के दिनों (में)
in the rainy season ([in] the days of the rainy season)	***barsāt ke dinõ (MẼ)**** बरसात के दिनों (में)

*The postposition here (***mẽ*** "in") may be omitted.

in 2014 (in the year two thousand and fourteen)	***san do hazār caudah MẼ*** सन् दो हज़ार चौदह में
in 2015	***san do hazār pandrah MẼ*** सन् दो हज़ार पंद्रह में
in the twenty-first century (f)	***ikkīsvī̃ śatabdī MẼ*** इक्कीसवीं शताब्दी में
on the first (date) (f)	***pehlī tārīkh KO*** पहली तारीख़ को
on the fifteen (date)	***pandrah tārīkh KO*** पंद्रह तारीख़ को
What is the date today?	***āj kī tārīkh kyā hai?*** आज की तारीख़ क्या है?
next/previous week	***agle/pichle hafte*** अगले/पिछले हफ़्ते
next/previous month	***agle/pichle mahīne*** अगले/पिछले महीने
next/previous year	***agle/pichle sāl*** अगले/पिछले साल
this/that week	***is/us hafte*** इस/उस हफ़्ते

this/that month	***is/us mahīne*** इस/उस महीने
this/that year	***is/us sāl*** इस/उस साल
after three months	***tīn hafte bād*** तीन हफ़्ते बाद
after two years	***do sāl bād*** दो साल बाद
three months ago	***tīn mahīne pehle*** तीन महीने पहले
at two o'clock	***do baje*** दो बजे

1.3 What time is it?

What is the time?	***kyā baj gayā?/ṭāim kyā hai?*** क्या बज गया?/टाइम क्या है?
It's nine o'clock. (nine have struck)	***nau baje haĩ.*** नौ बजे हैं।
It's one thirty. (1½ has struck)	***ḍeṛh bajā hai.*** डेढ़ बजा है।
It's two thirty. (2½ has struck)	***ḍhāī baje haĩ.*** ढाई बजे हैं।
It's three thirty. (3½ has struck)	***sāṛhe tīn baje haĩ.*** साढ़े तीन बजे हैं।
It's four thirty. (4½ has struck)	***sāṛhe cār baje haĩ.*** साढ़े चार बजे हैं।

NB: With the exception of 1:30 and 2:30, the word साढ़े ***sāṛhe*** (+ half) is employed with the number to express half-hour times.

It's one fifteen. (1¼ has struck)	***savā bajā hai.*** सवा बजा है।

It's two fifteen. (2¼ has struck)	***savā do baje haĩ.*** सवा दो बजे हैं।
It's three fifteen. (3¼ has struck)	***savā tīn baje haĩ.*** सवा तीन बजे हैं।

With the exception of 1:15, the word सवा ***savā*** (+ one-quarter) is employed with the number to express a time fifteen minutes past the hour.

It's twelve forty-five. (-¼ has struck)	***paun bajā hai.*** पौन बजा है।
It's one forty-five. (2¼ has struck)	***paune do baje haĩ.*** पौने दो बजे हैं।
It's two forty-five. (3¼ has struck)	***paune tīn baje haĩ.*** पौने तीन बजे हैं।

With the exception of 12:45, the word पौने ***paune*** (– one-quarter) is employed with the number to express a time fifteen minutes before the hour.

It's two ten. (having struck 2 there are 10 minutes)	***do baj kar das minaṭ hue haĩ.*** दो बज कर दस मिनट हुए हैं।
It's two twenty. (having struck 2 there are 20 minutes)	***do baj kar bīs minaṭ hue haĩ.*** दो बज कर बीस मिनट हुए हैं।
It's ten to two. (in striking 2 there are 10 minutes)	***do bajne mẽ das minaṭ haĩ.*** दो बजने में दस मिनट हैं।
It's twenty to two. (in striking 2 there are 20 minutes)	***do bajne mẽ bīs minaṭ haĩ.*** दो बजने में बीस मिनट हैं।
half an hour (m)	***ādhā ghaṇṭā*** आधा घंटा
in half an hour (after half an hour)	***ādhe ghaṇṭe bād*** आधे घंटे बाद

in two hours (after 2 hours)	***do ghaṇṭe bād*** दो घंटे बाद
two hours ago (2 hours previously)	***do ghaṇṭe pehle*** दो घंटे पहले

maĩ kitne baje āū̃? At what time may I come?
मैं कितने बजे आऊँ?
ḍhāī baje āiye. Please come at 2:30.
ढाई बजे आइये।
do baj kar bīs minaṭ par āiye. Please come at 2:20.
दो बज कर बीस मिनट पर आइये।
tīn bajne mẽ bīs minaṭ par āiye. Please come at 20 of 3.
तीन बजने में बीस मिनट पर आइये।

early	***jaldī*** जल्दी
late	***der se*** देर से
on time	***ṭhīk samay par*** ठीक समय पर

1.4 One, two, three...

one	***ek***	एक
two	***do***	दो
three	***tīn***	तीन
four	***cār***	चार
five	***pā̃c***	पाँच
six	***chai***	छै/छह/छः
seven	***sāt***	सात
eight	***āṭh***	आठ
nine	***nau***	नौ

ten	***das***	दस
eleven	***gyārah***	ग्यारह
twelve	***bārah***	बारह
thirteen	***terah***	तेरह
fourteen	***caudah***	चौदह
fifteen	***pandrah***	पंद्रह
sixteen	***solah***	सोलह
seventeen	***satrah***	सत्रह
eighteen	***aṭhārah***	अठारह
nineteen	***unnīs***	उन्नीस
twenty	***bīs***	बीस
twenty-one	***ikkīs***	इक्कीस
twenty-two	***bāīs***	बाईस
twenty-three	***teīs***	तेईस
twenty-four	***caubīs***	चौबीस
twenty-five	***paccīs***	पच्चीस
twenty-six	***chabbīs***	छब्बीस
twenty-seven	***sattāīs***	सत्ताईस
twenty-eight	***aṭṭhāīs***	अट्ठाईस
twenty-nine	***untīs***	उनतीस
thirty	***tīs***	तीस
thirty-one	***ikattīs***	इकत्तीस
thirty-two	***battīs***	बत्तीस
thirty-three	***taĩtīs***	तैंतीस
thirty-four	***caũtīs***	चौंतीस
thirty-five	***paĩtīs***	पैंतीस
thirty-six	***chattīs***	छत्तीस
thirty-seven	***saĩtīs***	सैंतीस
thirty-eight	***aṛtīs***	अड़तीस
thirty-nine	***untālīs***	उनतालीस
forty	***cālīs***	चालीस

forty-one	***iktālīs***	इकतालीस
forty-two	***bayālīs***	बयालीस
forty-three	***taĩtālīs***	तैंतालीस
forty-four	***cavālīs***	चवालीस
forty-five	***paĩtālīs***	पैंतालीस
forty-six	***chiyālīs***	छियालीस
forty-seven	***saĩtālīs***	सैंतालीस
forty-eight	***aṛtālīs***	अड़तालीस
forty-nine	***uncās***	उनचास
fifty	***pacās***	पचास
fifty one	***ikyāvan***	इक्यावन
fifty-two	***bāvan***	बावन
fifty-three	***tirpan***	तिरपन
fifty-four	***cauvan***	चौवन
fifty-five	***pacpan***	पचपन
fifty-six	***chappan***	छप्पन
fifty-seven	***sattāvan***	सत्तावन
fifty-eight	***aṭṭhāvan***	अट्ठावन
fifty-nine	***unsaṭh***	उनसठ
sixty	***sāṭh***	साठ
sixty-one	***iksaṭh***	इकसठ
sixty-two	***bāsaṭh***	बासठ
sixty-three	***tirsaṭh***	तिरसठ
sixty-four	***caũsaṭh***	चौंसठ
sixty-five	***paĩsaṭh***	पैंसठ
sixty-six	***chiyāsaṭh***	छियासठ
sixty-seven	***saṛsaṭh***	सड़सठ
sixty-eight	***aṛsaṭh***	अड़सठ
sixty-nine	***unhattar***	उनहत्तर
seventy	***sattar***	सत्तर
seventy-one	***ikhattar***	इकहत्तर

seventy-two	***bahattar***	बहत्तर
seventy-three	***tihattar***	तिहत्तर
seventy-four	***cauhattar***	चौहत्तर
seventy-five	***pachattar***	पचहत्तर
seventy-six	***chihattar***	छिहत्तर
seventy-seven	***sathattar***	सतहत्तर
seventy-eight	***aṭhhattar***	अठहत्तर
seventy-nine	***unāsī***	उनासी
eighty	***assī***	अस्सी
eighty-one	***ikyāsī***	इक्यासी
eighty-two	***bayāsī***	बयासी
eighty-three	***tirāsī***	तिरासी
eighty-four	***caurāsī***	चौरासी
eighty-five	***pacāsī***	पचासी
eighty-six	***chiyāsī***	छियासी
eighty-seven	***sattāsī***	सत्तासी
eighty-eight	***aṭhāsī/aṭṭhāsī***	अठासी/अट्ठासी
eighty-nine	***navāsī***	नवासी
ninety	***nabbe***	नब्बे
ninety-one	***ikyānve***	इक्यानवे
ninety-two	***bānve/bayānve***	बानवे/बयानवे
ninety-three	***tirānve***	तिरानवे
ninety-four	***caurānve***	चौरानवे
ninety-five	***pacānve***	पचानवे
ninety-six	***chiyānve***	छियानवे
ninety-seven	***sattānve***	सत्तानवे
ninety-eight	***aṭṭhānve***	अट्ठानवे
ninety-nine	***ninyānve***	निन्यानवे
one hundred	***sau***	सौ
101	***ek sau ek***	एक सौ एक
200	***do sau***	दो सौ

1000	***hazār/sahasra***	हज़ार/सहस्र
1001	***ek hazār ek***	एक हज़ार एक
2000	***do hazār***	दो हज़ार
100,000 (written 1,00,000 in India)	***lākh***	लाख
101,000 (written 1,01,000)	***ek lākh ek hazār***	एक लाख, एक हज़ार
10,000,000 (written 1,00,00,000)	***karoṛ***	करोड़
10,100,000 (written 1,01,00,000)	***ek karoṛ ek lākh***	एक करोड़, एक लाख
1,000,000,000	***arab***	अरब

Ordinal Numbers

first	***pehlā/pratham***	पहला/प्रथम*
second	***dūsrā/dvitīya***	दूसरा/द्वितीय*
third	***tīsrā/tṛtīyā***	तीसरा/तृतीय*
fourth	***cauthā/caturth***	चौथा/चतुर्थ*
fifth	***pā̃cvā̃***	पाँचवाँ
sixth	***chaṭhā***	छठा
seventh	***sātvā̃***	सातवाँ
eighth	***āṭhvā̃***	आठवाँ
ninth	***navā̃***	नवाँ
tenth	***dasvā̃***	दसवाँ

From ten onwards, the adjectival suffix -वाँ ***-vā̃*** is added to the cardinal number.

* The words with astericks next to them are words from Sanskrit that are employed in formal Hindi.

The following are symbols that represent the digits from 0 to 9. They are actually the basis of the "Arabic" numerals used in English. Both sets of numerals are commonly encountered in Hindi.

०	१	२	३	४	५	६	७	८	९
0	1	2	3	4	5	6	7	8	9

There are 100 paise in a rupee.	***ek rupaye mẽ sau paise hote haĩ.*** एक रुपये में सौ पैसे होते हैं।
I have one 101 rupees. (near me there are 101 rupees)	***mere pās ek sau ek rupaye haĩ.*** मेरे पास एक सौ एक रुपये हैं।

1.5 The weather

How will today's weather be?	***āj kā mausam kaisā hogā?*** आज का मौसम कैसा होगा?
How will tomorrow's weather be?	***kal kā mausam kaisā hogā?*** कल का मौसम कैसा होगा?
Will today's weather be bad?	***kyā āj kā mausam kharāb rahegā?*** क्या आज मौसम ख़राब रहेगा?
Today's weather is (very) bad.	***kyā āj kā mausam (bahut) kharāb hai.*** आज का मौसम (बहुत) ख़राब है।
Today's weather is (very) good.	***kyā āj kā mausam (bahut) acchā hai.*** आज का मौसम (बहुत) अच्छा है।
Will it rain today?	***kyā āj bāriś hogī?*** क्या आज बारिश होगी?
It is raining (a lot) today.	***āj (bahut) bāriś ho rahī hai.*** आज (बहुत) बारिश हो रही है।
Will it be (very) hot today?	***kyā āj (bahut) garmī hogī?*** क्या आज बहुत गर्मी होगी?
It is (very) hot today.	***āj (bahut) garmī ho rahī hai.*** आज बहुत गर्मी हो रही है।
Will it be (very) cold today?	***kyā āj (bahut) ṭhaṇḍ hogī?*** क्या आज बहुत ठंड होगी?
It is (very) cold today	***āj (bahut) ṭhaṇḍ ho rahī hai.*** आज बहुत ठंड हो रही है।

What will be the temperature today? **āj tāpmān kyā hogā?** आज तापमान क्या होगा?

Will there be fog today? **kyā āj kuhrā hogā?** क्या आज कुहरा होगा?

Will there be humidity today? **āj kyā umas hogī?** आज क्या उमस होगी?

humidity (f) **umas** उमस	breeze (m) **bayār** बयार	light rain (f) **bū̃dābā̃dī** बूँदाबाँदी
snow/ice (f) **barf** बर्फ़	wind (f) **havā** हवा	a clear sky (m) **sāf āsmān** साफ़ आसमान
rain (f) **bāriś** बारिश	high wind (f) **tez havā** तेज़ हवा	a gray sky (m) **gandlā āsmān** गंदला आसमान
harsh sunlight (f) **tez dhūp** तेज़ धूप	a hot wind (f) **lū** लू	clouds (m) **bādal** बादल
warm (sweet) sunlight (f) **mīṭhī dhūp** मीठी धूप	an icy wind (f) **barfīlī havā** बर्फ़ीली हवा	very hot (much heat) (f) **bahut garmī** बहुत गर्मी
dew (f) **os/śabnam** ओस/शबनम	heavy rain (f) **mūslādhār bāriś** मूसलाधार बारिश	very cold (much cold) (f) **bahut ṭhaṇḍ** बहुत ठंड
hail stones (m, pl) **ole** ओले	a storm (f) **ā̃dhī** आँधी	fog (m) **kuhrā** कुहरा
temperature (m) **tāpmān** तापमान	minimum temperature (m) **nyūntam tāpmān** न्यूनतम तापमान	maximum temperature (m) **adhiktam tāpmān** अधिकतम तापमान

1.6 Here, there...

here, over here/there, over there	***yahā̃/vahā̃*** यहाँ/वहाँ
hither/thither	***idhar/udhar*** इधर/उधर
where	***kahā̃*** कहाँ
somewhere/nowhere	***kahī̃/kahī̃ nahī̃*** कहीं/कहीं नहीं
anywhere at all	***kahī̃ bhī*** कहीं भी
(very) far	***(bahut) dūr*** (बहुत) दूर
(very) close	***(bahut) nazdīk/pās*** (बहुत) नज़दीक/पास
on the right side	***dāhinī taraf/or*** दाहिनी तरफ़/ओर
on the left side	***bāyī̃ taraf/or*** बायीं तरफ़/ओर
straight ahead	***sīdhe*** सीधे
in all four directions	***cārõ taraf/or*** चारों तरफ़/ओर
ahead/ahead of x	***āge/x ke āge*** आगे/x के आगे
behind/behind x	***pīche/x ke pīche*** पीछे/x के पीछे
above/above x	***ūpar/x ke ūpar*** ऊपर/x के ऊपर
below/below x	***nīce/x ke nīce*** नीचे/x के नीचे

outside/outside x	***bāhar/x ke bāhar*** बाहर/x के बाहर
inside/inside x	***andar/x ke andar*** अंदर/x के अंदर
in	***mẽ*** में
on	***par/pe*** पर/पे
from, by, with	***se*** से
next to/near x	***pās/x ke pās*** पास/x के पास
previously	***pehle*** पहले
before/before x	***pehle/x se pehle*** पहले/x से पहले
first of all	***sab se pehle*** सब से पहले
afterwards/after x	***bād mẽ/x ke bād*** बाद में/x के बाद
in the middle/in the middle of x	***bīc mẽ/x ke bīc mẽ*** बीच में/x के बीच में
via x	***x se ho kar*** x से होकर
north (m)/in the north	***uttar/uttar mẽ*** उत्तर/उत्तर में
south (m)/in the south	***dakṣiṇ/dakṣin mẽ*** दक्षिण/दक्षिण में
east (m)/in the east	***pūrv/pūrv mẽ*** पूर्व/पूर्व में
west (m) /in the west	***paścim/paścim mẽ*** पश्चिम/पश्चिम में

1.7 What does that sign say?

drinking water (m)
pīne kā pānī
पीने का पानी

No Smoking
dhūmrapān karnā niṣedh hai
धूम्रपान करना निषेध है।

No Entry
andar jānā manā hai
अंदर जाना मना है।

Stop
ṭhehriye
ठहरिये

Men at Work
ādmī kām par haĩ
आदमी काम पर हैं।

Public toilet (m)
sārvajanik śaucālay
सार्वजनिक शौचालय

Drive slowly (move slowly)
dhīre caliye
धीरे चलिये

Use the horn
hārn dījiye
हॉर्न दीजिये

Remain quiet
śānt rehẽ
शांत रहें

Speed limit (f)
gati sīmā
गति सीमा

Speed hump (m) (speed breaker)
gati avarodhak
गति अवरोधक

Police (f)
pulis
पुलिस

Danger (m)
khatrā
ख़तरा

Keep left
bāyī̃ taraf calẽ
बायीं तरफ़ चलें

Remain vigilant
sāvadhān rahẽ
सावधान रहें

Airport (m)
havāī aḍḍā
हवाई अड्डा

Fixed price (m)
ek dām
एक दाम

Please take off your shoes
jūte utārẽ
जूते उतारें

Please switch off your mobile.
mobāil band rakhẽ
मोबाइल बंद रखें

It is forbidden to urinate here.
yahā̃ peśāb karnā manā hai.
यहाँ पेशाब करना मना है।

Men
puruṣ
पुरुष

Women
mahilāẽ
महिलाएँ

No parking
yahā̃ gāṛī khaṛī karnā manā hai.
यहाँ गाड़ी खड़ी करना मना है।

1.8 Legal holidays

Many of the observed holidays in India surround religious festivals for the various religions in India, including those for Hinduism, Islam, and Christianity. The three most important national secular holidays are Independence Day (15 August), Republic Day (26 January), and Gandhi Jayanti (Mahatma Gandhi's birthday, 2 October). Other religious holidays are celebrated more regionally.

Divali ***divālī*** दिवाली

The Hindu festival of light. This is observed in October/November, and celebrates the change of season and the victory of light over darkness.

Holi ***holī*** होली

The Hindu festival of colors. This festival is observed in March/April and celebrates the changing of the seasons and victory over the demoness Holika.

Raksha Bandhan ***rakṣā bandhan*** रक्षा बंधन

On this occasion sisters tie a string around the wrist of their brothers as a sign that they will protect them. It is celebrated in July/August.

Dussehra ***daśehrā*** दशहरा

This is a significant Hindu festival celebrated in October that marks the victory of Lord Rama over Ravana in Lanka from the epic poem the *Ramayana*, as well as in honor of the Goddess Durga.

Eid ***īd*** ईद

Eid or Eid-ul-fitr is the principal Muslim festival in South Asia, and is celebrated to mark the end of the month of Ramadan when Muslims fast during the day for thirty days.

Muharram ***muharram*** मुहर्रम

This festvial is one of the most important Muslim festivals in South Asia, and is observed by Shia Muslims to remember the martyrdom of the grandson of the prophet Muhammad, Imam Hussain.

Christmas ***baṛā din/khriṣṭ jayantī*** बड़ा दिन/ख्रीष्ट जयंती

The most important celebration for Christians marking the birth of Jesus Christ.

New Year ***nayā sāl/nav varṣ*** नया साल/नव वर्ष

This is celebrated in India with increasing fervor. There are new year celebrations according to other calendars in India, but the celebration at the end of December is gradually becoming more significant.

Independence Day ***svatantratā divas*** स्वतंत्रता दिवस

This holiday marks the day India became independent from Britain on 15 August, 1947.

Republic Day ***gaṇtantra divas*** गणतंत्र दिवस

This holiday marks the day that India became a republic and the new constitution came into effect in India on 26 January, 1950.

Gandhi Jayanti ***gāndhī jayantī*** गांधी जयंती

This national holiday marks the birthday of one of India's most famous nationalist leaders, Mohandas Karamchand Gandhi, who was born on 2 October, 1869.

2 Meet and Greet

2. Meet and Greet

2.1 Greetings

good morning	***suprabhāt*** सुप्रभात
good night	***śubh rātri*** शुभ रात्रि
hello/goodbye	***namaste*** नमस्ते
hello/goodbye	***namaskār*** नमस्कार
How are you (m/f)?	***āp kaise/kaisī haĩ?*** आप कैसे/कैसी हैं?
I am fine.	***maĩ ṭhīk hū̃.*** मैं ठीक हूँ।
Fine, how are you? (enough, you relate)	***bas, āp sunāiye.*** बस, आप सुनाइये।
See you again. ([we] will meet again)	***[ham] phir milẽge.*** [हम] फिर मिलेंगे।
Okay, I'm off. (m/f) (Good, I move)	***acchā, maĩ caltā/caltī hū̃.*** अच्छा, मैं चलता/चलती हूँ।
May I go? (please give permission)	***ijāzat dījiye.*** इजाज़त दीजिये।
See you later. (will meet after)	***bād mẽ milẽge.*** बाद में मिलेंगे।
Go well.	***acche se jāiye.*** अच्छे से जाइये।
Have a safe trip. (arrive safely)	***sahī-salāmat pahũciye.*** सही-सलामत पहुँचिये।

It has been a pleasure meeting you. (having met you much happiness happened)	***āpse mil kar bahut <u>kh</u>uśī huī.*** आपसे मिलकर बहुत ख़ुशी हुई।
Likewise. (to me as well)	***mujhe bhī.*** मुझे भी।
Have a good trip. (auspicious journey)	***śubh yātrā.*** शुभ यात्रा।

2.2 Asking a question

yes	***jī hā̃*** जी हाँ
no	***jī nahī̃*** जी नहीं
What is this?	***yeh kyā hai?*** यह क्या है?
What is that?	***voh kyā hai?*** वह क्या है?
What are these?	***ye kyā haĩ?*** ये क्या हैं?
What are those?	***vo kyā haĩ?*** वे क्या हैं?
Is this …?	***kyā yeh … hai?*** क्या यह … है?
Is that …?	***kyā voh … hai?*** क्या वह … है?
Are these …?	***kyā ye … haĩ?*** क्या ये … हैं?
Are those …?	***kyā vo … haĩ?*** क्या वे … हैं?
Who is this? (polite)	***ye kaun haĩ?*** ये कौन हैं?

Who is that? (polite)	***vo kaun haĩ?*** वे कौन हैं?
Who are you? (polite)	***āp kaun haĩ?*** आप कौन हैं?
Who are you? (informal)	***tum kaun ho?*** तुम कौन हो?
What is your (good) name? (polite)	***āpkā (śubh) nām kyā hai?*** आपका (शुभ) नाम क्या है?
What is your name? (informal)	***tumhārā nām kyā hai?*** तुम्हारा नाम क्या है?
What is his/her name? (polite, close)	***inkā nām kyā hai?*** इनका नाम क्या है?
What is his/her name? (polite, far)	***unkā nām kyā hai?*** उनका नाम क्या है?
What is his/her name? (informal, close)	***iskā nām kyā hai?*** इसका नाम क्या है?
What is his/her name? (informal, far)	***uskā nām kyā hai?*** उसका नाम क्या है?
What do you do? (m/f) (polite)	***āp kyā karte/kartī haĩ?*** आप क्या करते/करती हैं?
What do you do? (m/f) (informal)	***tum kyā karte/kartī ho?*** तुम क्या करते/करती हो?
What does he/she do? (m/f) (polite, close)	***ye kyā karte/kartī haĩ?*** ये क्या करते/करती हैं?
What does he/she do? (m/f) (polite, far)	***vo kyā karte/kartī haĩ?*** वे क्या करते/करती हैं?
What does he/she do? (m/f) (informal, close)	***yeh kyā kartā/kartī hai?*** यह क्या करता/करती है?
What does he/she do? (m/f) (informal, far)	***voh kyā kartā/kartī hai?*** वह क्या करता/करती है?
What do [they] call this?	***ise kyā kehte haĩ?*** इसे क्या कहते हैं?

My name is	***merā nām ... hai.*** मेरा नाम ... है।
[They] call this a	***ise ... kehte haĩ.*** इसे ... कहते हैं।
When will we go?	***ham kab jāẽge?*** हम कब जाएँगे?
Where will we go?	***ham kahā̃ jāẽge?*** हम कहाँ जाएँगे?
How will we go? (in what manner)	***ham kaise jāẽge?*** हम कैसे जाएँगे?
Will we go by car?	***kyā ham cār se jāẽge?*** क्या हम कार से जाएँगे?
Will we go by train?	***kyā ham ṭren se jāẽge?*** क्या हम ट्रेन से जाएँगे?
What time will we go?	***ham kitne baje jāẽge?*** हम कितने बजे जाएँगे?
Where are you from? (m/f) (polite)	***āp kahā̃ ke/kī haĩ?*** आप कहाँ के/की हैं?
Where are you from (of)? (m/f) (informal)	***tum kahā̃ ke/kī ho?*** तुम कहाँ के/की हो?
How far is that from here?	***voh yahā̃ se kitnī dūr hai?*** वह यहाँ से कितनी दूर है?
Is that very far from here?	***kyā voh yahā̃ se bahut dūr hai?*** क्या वह यहाँ से बहुत दूर है?
May I help you? (may I do your help)	***kyā maĩ āpkī madad karū̃?*** क्या मैं आपकी मदद करूँ?
Can you help me? (m/f) (will you do my help)	***kyā āp merī madad karẽge/karẽgī?*** क्या आप मेरी मदद करेंगे/करेंगी?
Will you take tea/coffee? (m/f)	***kyā āp cāī/kāfī lẽge/lẽgī?*** क्या आप चाय/कॉफ़ी लेंगे/लेंगी?
Do you have a ...?	***kyā āpke pās ... ?*** क्या आपके पास ... है?

How much is this? (m/f) (of how much is this)	***yeh kitne kā/kī hai?*** यह कितने का/की है?
What is the price of this?	***iskā dām kyā hai?*** इसका दाम क्या है?
What is your age?	***āpkī umr kyā hai?*** आपकी उम्र क्या है?
Is your age of (twenty) years?	***kyā āpkī umr (bīs) sāl kī hai?*** क्या आपकी उम्र (बीस) साल की है?
Do you know English?	***kyā āp ko angrezī ātī hai?*** क्या आपको अंग्रेज़ी आती है?
How many brothers and sisters do you have?	***āpke kitne bhāī-behn haĩ?*** आपके कितने भाई-बहन हैं?
Is your brother older (bigger) than you?	***kyā āpke bhāī āpse baṛe haĩ?*** क्या आपके भाई आपसे बड़े हैं?
Is your brother younger (smaller) than you?	***kyā āpke bhāī āpse choṭe haĩ?*** क्या आपके भाई आपसे छोटे हैं?
Is your sister older (bigger) than you?	***kyā āpkī behn āpse baṛī hai?*** क्या आपकी बहन आपसे बड़ी है?
Is your sister younger (smaller) than you?	***kyā āpkī behn āpse choṭī hai?*** क्या आपकी बहन आपसे छोटी है?

2.3 Answering a question

yes	***jī hā̃*** जी हाँ
no	***jī nahī̃*** जी नहीं
yes, of course (certainly)!	***jī hā̃, zarūr!*** जी हाँ, ज़रूर!
I don't know. (to me is not known)	***mujhe mālūm nahī̃ (hai).*** मुझे मालूम नहीं (है)।

I don't remember. (to me memory is not)	***mujhe yād nahī̃ (hai).*** मुझे याद नहीं (है)।
I am okay.	***maĩ ṭhīk hū̃.*** मैं ठीक हूँ।
I am perfectly fine. (I am in enjoyment)	***maĩ maze mẽ hū̃.*** मैं मज़े में हूँ।
I have one brother.	***merā ek bhāī hai.*** मेरा एक भाई है।
I have two brothers.	***mere do bhāī haĩ.*** मेरे दो भाई हैं।
I have one sister.	***merī ek behn hai.*** मेरी एक बहन है।
I have three sisters.	***merī tīn behnẽ haĩ.*** मेरी तीन बहनें हैं।
I don't have any brother or sister.	***merā koī bhāī-behn nahī̃ hai.*** मेरा कोई भाई-बहन नहीं है।
My brother is older than I am.	***merā bhāī mujhse baṛā hai.*** मेरा भाई मुझसे बड़ा है।
My brother is younger than I am.	***merā bhāī mujhse choṭā hai.*** मेरा भाई मुझसे छोटा है।
I am older than my sister. (m/f)	***maĩ apnī behn se baṛā/baṛī hū̃.*** मैं अपनी बहन से बड़ा/बड़ी हूँ।
I am younger than my sister. (m/f)	***maĩ apnī behn se choṭā/choṭī hū̃.*** मैं अपनी बहन से छोटा/छोटी हूँ।

2.4 Thank you

Thank you.	***śukriyā.*** शुक्रिया।
Thank you very much.	***bahut śukriyā.*** बहुत शुक्रिया।

Thank you very very much.	***bahut bahut śukriyā.***	बहुत बहुत शुक्रिया।
Not a problem. ([it's] no matter)	***koī bāt nahī̃.***	कोई बात नहीं।
I am very grateful.	***maĩ bahut ehsānmand hū̃.***	मैं बहुत एहसानमंद हूँ।
Pardon me. (please listen)	***suniye.***	सुनिये।
Would you help me? (m/f) (polite) (will you do my help)	***kyā āp merī madad karẽge/karẽgī?***	क्या आप मेरी मदद करेंगे/करेंगी?
Would you help me? (m/f) (informal) (will you do my help)	***kyā tum merī madad karoge/karogī?***	क्या तुम मेरी मदद करोगे/करोगी?
Would you come with me? (m/f) (polite)	***kyā āp mere sāth āẽge/āẽgī?***	क्या आप मेरे साथ आएँगे/आएँगी?
Would you come with me? (m/f) (informal)	***kyā tum mere sāth āoge/āogī?***	क्या तुम मेरे साथ आओगे/आओगी?
May I help you? (may I do your help)	***maĩ āp kī madad karū̃?***	मैं आपकी मदद करूँ?
May I come with you?	***maĩ āpke sāth āū̃?***	मैं आपके साथ आऊँ?
Thank you for the tea/coffee/soda.	***cāy/kāfī/soḍā ke liye śukriyā.***	चाय/कॉफ़ी/सोडा के लिये शुक्रिया।
Thank you for coming.	***āne ke liye śukriyā.***	आने के लिये शुक्रिया।
Thank you for the help. (for doing help)	***madad karne ke liye śukriyā.***	मदद करने के लिये शुक्रिया।
Thank you for showing (me).	***dikhāne ke liye śukriyā.***	दिखाने के लिये शुक्रिया।
I really liked the food. (to me the food was much preferred)	***mujhe yeh khānā bahut pasand āyā.***	मुझे यह खाना बहुत पसंद आया।

I really liked the tea.	***mujhe cāy bahut acchī lagī/pasand āyī.*** मुझे चाय बहुत अच्छी लगी/पसंद आयी।

2.5 I'm sorry

Please forgive me.	***mujhe māf kījiye.*** मुझे माफ़ कीजिये।
I am sorry to hear this. (having heard this much sorrow happened)	***yeh sunkar bahut afsos huā.*** यह सुनकर बहुत अफ़सोस हुआ।
This is terrible. (a bad thing)	***yeh bahut burī bāt hai.*** यह बहुत बुरी बात है।
I didn't know this.	***yeh mujhe mālūm nahī̃ thā.*** यह मुझे मालूम नहीं था।
It will not happen a second time.	***dubārā nahī̃ hogā.*** दुबारा नहीं होगा।
It is no concern. (no matter of concern)	***cintā kī koī bāt nahī̃ (hai).*** चिंता की कोई बात नहीं (है)।
No matter.	***koī bāt nahī̃.*** कोई बात नहीं।

2.6 What do you think?

What is your opinion? (what is your thought)	***āpkā kyā khyāl/vicār hai?*** आपका क्या ख़्याल/विचार है?
What is your opinion?	***āpkī kyā rāy hai?*** आपकी क्या राय है?
What is your opinion in this matter?	***is māmle mẽ āpkā kyā khyāl/vicār hai?*** इस मामले में आपका क्या ख़्याल/विचार है?

What is your opinion about this?	***is bāre mẽ āpkā kyā <u>kh</u>yāl/vicār hai?*** इस बारे में आपका क्या ख़्याल/विचार है?
What do you think? (m/f) (polite)	***āp kyā socte/soctī haĩ?*** आप क्या सोचते/सोचती हैं?
What do you think? (m/f) (informal)	***tum kyā socte/soctī ho?*** तुम क्या सोचते/सोचती हो?
Congratulations!	***badhāī ho!*** बधाई हो!
Well done! (to children)	***śābāś!*** शाबाश!
In my opinion…	***mere <u>kh</u>yāl mẽ…*** मेरे ख़्याल में...
I think that… (m/f)	***maĩ soctā/soctī hū̃ ki…*** मैं सोचता/सोचती हूँ कि ...
I believe that… (to me the belief is that…)	***mujhe yaqīn hai ki …*** मुझे यक़ीन है कि ...
This is very good.	***yeh bahut acchā hai.*** यह बहुत अच्छा है।
This is not good.	***yeh acchā nahī̃ hai.*** यह अच्छा नहीं है।
This is very bad.	***yeh bahut <u>kh</u>arāb/burā hai.*** यह बहुत ख़राब/बुरा है।
This went (happened) well.	***yeh bahut acchā huā.*** यह बहुत अच्छा हुआ।
This went (happened) badly.	***yeh bahut <u>kh</u>arāb/burā huā.*** यह बहुत ख़राब/बुरा हुआ।
This will be (happen) great.	***yeh bahut acchā hogā.*** यह बहुत अच्छा होगा।
This will be (happen) very bad.	***yeh bahut <u>kh</u>arāb/burā hogā.*** यह बहुत ख़राब/बुरा होगा।

I am very happy.	***maĩ bahut <u>kh</u>uś hū̃.*** मैं बहुत ख़ुश हूँ।
I am very sad.	***maĩ bahut dukhī hū̃.*** मैं बहुत दुखी हूँ।
Are you happy? (polite)	***kyā āp <u>kh</u>uś haĩ?*** क्या आप ख़ुश हैं?
Are you sad? (polite)	***kyā āp dukhī haĩ?*** क्या आप दुखी हैं?
I am very worried.	***maĩ bahut fikramand hū̃.*** मैं बहुत फ़िक्रमंद हूँ।
What happened?	***kyā huā?*** क्या हुआ?
Nothing happened.	***kuch nahī̃ huā!*** कुछ नहीं हुआ।
What is happening?	***kyā ho rahā hai?*** क्या हो रहा है?
What will happen?	***kyā hogā?*** क्या होगा?
What was happening?	***kyā ho rahā thā?*** क्या हो रहा था?
Why is this happening?	***yeh kyõ ho rahā hai?*** यह क्यों हो रहा है?
Why did this happen?	***yeh/aisā kyõ huā?*** यह/ऐसा क्यों हुआ?
When will this happen?	***yeh/aisā kab hogā?*** यह/ऐसा कब होगा?

3 Small Talk

3. Small Talk

3.1 Introductions

Hello/Goodbye	***namaste*** नमस्ते
What is your (good) name?	***āpkā śubh nām kyā hai?*** आपका शुभ नाम क्या है?
I am …	***maĩ … hū̃.*** मैं … हूँ।
My name is …	***merā nām … hai.*** मेरा नाम … है।
This is my wife. (polite)	***ye merī patnī hai.*** ये मेरी पत्नी हैं।
Her name is … (polite)	***inkā nām … hai.*** इनका नाम … है।
This is my husband. (polite)	***ye mere pati haĩ.*** ये मेरे पति हैं।
His name is …. (polite)	***inkā nām … hai.*** इनका नाम … है।
This is my son/boy.	***yeh merā beṭā/laṛkā hai.*** यह मेरा बेटा/लड़का है।
His name is …	***iskā nām … hai.*** इसका नाम … है।
This is my daughter/girl.	***yeh merī beṭī/laṛkī hai.*** यह मेरी बेटी/लड़की है।
Her name is …	***iskā nām … hai.*** इसका नाम … है।
How many children do you have? (polite)	***āpke kitne bacce haĩ?*** आपके कितने बच्चे हैं?
How many children do you have? (informal)	***tumhāre kitne bacce haĩ?*** तुम्हारे कितने बच्चे हैं?

Do you have children? (polite)	***kyā āpke bāl-bacce haĩ?*** क्या आपके बाल-बच्चे हैं?
Do you have children? (informal)	***kyā tumhāre bacce haĩ?*** क्या तुम्हारे बच्चे हैं?
I don't have children. (any child)	***merā koī bāl-baccā nahĩ hai.*** मेरा कोई बाल-बच्चा नहीं है।
I have one child.	***merā ek baccā hai.*** मेरा एक बच्चा है।
I have (three) children.	***mere (tīn) bacce haĩ.*** मेरे (तीन) बच्चे हैं।
We have (three) children.	***hamāre (tīn) bacce haĩ.*** हमारे (तीन) बच्चे हैं।
I have one son/boy.	***merā ek beṭā/laṛkā hai.*** मेरा एक बेटा/लड़का है।
We have one daughter/girl.	***hamārī ek beṭī/laṛkī hai.*** मेरी एक बेटी/लड़की है।
We have (two) sons/boys.	***hamāre (do) beṭe/laṛke haĩ.*** हमारे (दो) बेटे/लड़के हैं।
I have (four) daughters/girls.	***merī (cār) beṭiyā̃/laṛkiyā̃ haĩ.*** मेरी (चार) बेटियाँ/लड़कियाँ हैं।
Are you married? (polite)	***kyā āp śādīśudā haĩ?*** क्या आप शादीशुदा हैं?
Are you married? (informal)	***kyā tum śādīśudā ho?*** क्या तुम शादीशुदा हो?
I am married. (my wedding has happened)	***merī śādī ho gayī.*** मेरी शादी हो गयी।
I am (not) married.	***maĩ śādīśudā (nahĩ) hū̃.*** मैं शादीशुदा (नहीं) हूँ।
I am divorced.	***maĩ talāqśudā hū̃.*** मैं तलाक़शुदा हूँ।
I am a widow.	***maĩ vidhvā hū̃.*** मैं विधवा हूँ।

I am a widower.	**maĩ vidhur hū̃.**
	मैं विधुर हूँ।
These are (not) my parents.	**ye mere mātā-pitā (nahī̃) haĩ.**
	ये मेरे माता-पिता (नहीं) हैं।
This is (not) my friend. (m/f)	**yeh merā/merī dost (nahī̃) hai.**
	यह मेरा/मेरी दोस्त (नहीं) है।
Where do you live? (m/f) (polite)	**āp kahā̃ rehte/rehtī haĩ?**
	आप कहाँ रहते/रहती हैं?
Where do you live? (m/f) (informal)	**tum kahā̃ rehte/rehtī ho?**
	तुम कहाँ रहते/रहती हो?
I live in …. (m/f)	**maĩ … mẽ rehtā/rehtī hū̃.**
	मैं … में रहता/रहती हूँ।
My parents live in ….	**mere mātā-pitā … mẽ rehte haĩ.**
	मेरे माता-पिता … में रहते हैं।
Where are you from? (m/f)	**āp kahā̃ ke/kī rehnevāle/rehnevālī haĩ?**
	आप कहाँ के/की रहनेवाले/रहनेवाली हैं?
I am (not) from …. (m/f)	**maĩ … kā/kī rehnevālā/rehnevālī (nahī̃) hū̃.**
	मैं … का/की रहनेवाला/रहनेवाली (नहीं) हूँ।
I am (not) from (of) … (m/f)	**maĩ … kā/kī (nahī̃) hū̃.**
	मैं … का/की (नहीं) हूँ।
I am (not) American.	**maĩ amrīkī (nahī̃) hū̃.**
	मैं अमरीकी (नहीं) हूँ।
I am (not) Australian.	**maĩ āsṭreliyan (nahī̃) hū̃.**
	मैं ऑस्ट्रेलियन (नहीं) हूँ।
I live in …. (m/f)	**maĩ … mẽ rehtā/rehtī hū̃.**
	मैं … में रहता/रहती हूँ।
I do not live in …. (m/f)	**maĩ … mẽ nahī̃ rehtā/rehtī.**
	मैं … में नहीं रहता/रहती।
I live with a friend. (m/f)	**maĩ dost ke sāth rehtā/rehtī hū̃.**
	मैं दोस्त के साथ रहता/रहती हूँ।

I live with friends. (m/f)	***maĩ dostõ ke sāth rehtā/rehtī hū̃.***	मैं दोस्तों के साथ रहता/रहती हूँ।
I live alone. (m)	***maĩ akele rehtā hū̃.***	मैं अकेले रहता हूँ।
I live alone. (f)	***maĩ akele rehtī hū̃.***	मैं अकेले रहती हूँ।
I live with my parents. (m/f)	***maĩ apne mātā-pitā ke sāth rehtā/rehtī hū̃.***	मैं अपने माता-पिता के साथ रहता/रहती हूँ।
I live with my wife. (m/f)	***maĩ apnī patnī ke sāth rehtā/rehtī hū̃.***	मैं अपनी पत्नी के साथ रहता/रहती हूँ।
I live with my husband. (m/f)	***maĩ apne pati ke sāth rehtā/rehtī hū̃.***	मैं अपने पति के साथ रहता/रहती हूँ।
I live with my partner. (m/f) (companion)	***maĩ apne/apnī sāthī ke sāth rehtā/rehtī hū̃.***	मैं अपने साथी के साथ रहता/रहती हूँ।
I live with my children. (m/f)	***maĩ apne baccõ ke sāth rehtā/rehtī hū̃.***	मैं अपने बच्चों के साथ रहता/रहती हूँ।
I live with a man. (m/f)	***maĩ ek ādmī ke sāth rehtā/rehtī hū̃.***	मैं एक आदमी के साथ रहता/रहती हूँ।
I live with a woman. (m/f)	***maĩ ek aurat ke sāth rehtā/rehtī hū̃.***	मैं एक औरत के साथ रहता/रहती हूँ।
My country is (not) ….	***merā deś … (nahī̃) hai.***	मेरा देश … (नहीं) है।
I am with my husband.	***maĩ apne pati ke sāth hū̃.***	मैं अपने पति के साथ हूँ।
I am with my wife.	***maĩ apnī patnī ke sāth hū̃.***	मैं अपनी पत्नी के साथ हूँ।
I am with my friend.	***maĩ apne dost ke sāth hū̃.***	मैं अपने दोस्त के साथ हूँ।
I am with my friends.	***maĩ apne dostõ ke sāth hū̃.***	मैं अपने दोस्तों के साथ हूँ।

What do you do? (m/f) (polite)	**āp kyā karte/kartī haĩ?** आप क्या करते/करती हैं?
What do you do? (m/f) (informal)	**tum kyā karte/kartī ho?** तुम क्या करते/करती हो?
Do you work? (m/f) (polite)	**kyā āp kām karte/kartī haĩ?** क्या आप काम करते/करती हैं?
Do you work? (m/f) (informal)	**kyā tum kām karte/kartī ho?** क्या तुम काम करते/करती हो?
What work do you do? (m/f) (polite)	**āp kyā kām karte/kartī haĩ?** आप क्या काम करते/करती हैं?
What work do you do? (m/f) (informal)	**tum kyā kām karte/kartī ho?** तुम क्या काम करते/करती हो?
Do you do a job. (m/f) (polite) (for money)	**kyā āp naukrī karte/kartī haĩ.** क्या आप नौकरी करते/करती हैं?
Do you do a job. (m/f) (informal) (for money)	**kyā tum naukrī karte/kartī ho.** क्या तुम नौकरी करते/करती हो?
I don't work. (m/f)	**maĩ kām nahī̃ kartā/kartī.** मैं काम नहीं करता/करती।
I do a job. (m/f) (for money)	**maĩ naukrī kartā/kartī hū̃.** मैं नौकरी करता/करती हूँ।
I don't do a job. (m/f) (for money)	**maĩ naukrī nahī̃ kartā/kartī.** मैं नौकरी नहीं करता/करती।
I am unemployed.	**maĩ berozgār hū̃.** मैं बेरोज़गार हूँ।
Are you unemployed? (polite)	**kyā āp berozgār haĩ?** क्या आप बेरोज़गार हैं?
Are you unemployed? (informal)	**kyā tum berozgār ho?** क्या तुम बेरोज़गार हो?
I am (not) a teacher.	**maĩ ṭīcar (nahī̃) hū̃.** मैं टीचर (नहीं) हूँ।
I am (not) a doctor.	**maĩ ḍākṭar (nahī̃) hū̃.** मैं डॉक्टर (नहीं) हूँ।

I am (not) a student.	*maĩ chātra (nahī̃) hū̃.*	मैं छात्र (नहीं) हूँ।
I am (not) a tourist.	*maĩ paryaṭak (nahī̃) hū̃.*	मैं पर्यटक (नहीं) हूँ।
I work in (India). (m/f)	*maĩ (bhārat) mẽ kām kartā/kartī hū̃.*	मैं (भारत) में काम करता/करती हूँ।
I work in (an office). (m/f)	*maĩ (daftar) mẽ kām kartā/kartī hū̃.*	मैं (दफ़्तर) में काम करता/करती हूँ।
I work in (a factory). (m/f)	*maĩ (faikṭrī) mẽ kām kartā/kartī hū̃.*	मैं (फ़ैक्टरी) में काम करता/करती हूँ।
I study in (India). (m/f)	*maĩ (bhārat) mẽ paṛhtā/paṛhtī hū̃.*	मैं (भारत) में पढ़ता/पढ़ती हूँ।
I study Hindi in (India). (m/f)	*maĩ (bhārat) mẽ hindī paṛhtā/paṛhtī hū̃.*	मैं (भारत) में हिन्दी पढ़ता/पढ़ती हूँ।
My home is in	*merā ghar ... mẽ hai.*	मेरा घर ... में है।
Where is your home? (polite)	*āpkā ghar kahā̃ hai?*	आपका घर कहाँ है?
Where is your home? (informal)	*tumhārā ghar kahā̃ hai?*	तुम्हारा घर कहाँ है?
Where is your family's home? (polite)	*āpke parivār kā ghar kahā̃ hai?*	आपके परिवार का घर कहाँ है?
Where is your family's home? (informal)	*tumhāre parivār kā ghar kahā̃ hai?*	तुम्हारे परिवार का घर कहाँ है?
How old are you? (m/f) (polite) (of how many years are you)	*āp kitne sāl ke/kī haĩ?*	आप कितने साल के/की हैं?
How old are you? (m/f) (informal) (of how many years are you)	*tum kitne sāl ke/kī ho?*	तुम कितने साल के/की हो?
I am (thirty) years. (m/f) (of thirty years)	*maĩ (tīs) sāl kā/kī hū̃.*	मैं (तीस) साल का/की हूँ।

3.2 I beg your pardon?

I know a little Hindi. (to me a little Hindi comes)	***mujhe thoṛī hindī ātī hai.*** मुझे थोड़ी हिन्दी आती है।
I don't know Hindi. (Hindi doesn't comes)	***mujhe hindī nahī̃ ātī.*** मुझे हिंदी नहीं आती।
I speak a little Hindi. (m/f)	***maĩ thoṛī hindī boltā/boltī hū̃.*** मैं थोड़ी हिन्दी बोलता/बोलती हूँ।
I don't speak Hindi. (m/f)	***maĩ hindī nahī̃ boltā/boltī.*** मैं हिंदी नहीं बोलता/बोलती।
I write Hindi. (m/f)	***maĩ hindī likhtā/likhtī hū̃.*** मैं हिन्दी लिखता/लिखती हूँ।
I don't write Hindi. (m/f)	***maĩ hindī nahī̃ likhtā/likhtī.*** मैं हिंदी नहीं लिखता/लिखती।
Pardon me! (said to gain attention)	***suniye!*** सुनिये!
Do you speak English? (m/f) (polite)	***kyā āp angrezī bolte/boltī haĩ?*** क्या आप अंग्रेज़ी बोलते/बोलती हैं?
Do you know English? (m/f) (polite)	***kyā āp angrezī jānte/jāntī haĩ?*** क्या आप अंग्रेज़ी जानते/जानती हैं?
I don't understand. (m/f)	***maĩ nahī̃ samajhtā/samajhtī.*** मैं नहीं समझता/समझती।
Please speak again.	***phir se kahiye.*** फिर से कहिये।
Please speak slowly.	***dhīre dhīre boliye.*** धीरे धीरे बोलिये।

is kā matlab kyā hai?
इसका मतलब क्या है?

What does this mean? (what is the meaning of this)

us kā matlab kyā hai? उसका मतलब क्या है?	What does that mean?
angrezī mẽ is kā matlab kyā hai? अंग्रेज़ी में इसका मतलब क्या है?	What is the meaning of this in English?
hindī mẽ ... ko kyā kehte haĩ? हिन्दी में ... को क्या कहते हैं?	What do they call ... in Hindi?
hindī mẽ ise kyā kehte haĩ? हिन्दी में इसे क्या कहते हैं?	What do they call this in Hindi?
zarā likhiye. ज़रा लिखिये।	Please write this down.
hindī mẽ ise kaise likhte haĩ? हिन्दी में इसे कैसे लिखते हैं?	How do they write this in Hindi?

Please wait (a moment).	***zarā rukiye.*** ज़रा रुकिये।
Please tell me.	***zarā mujhe batāiye.*** ज़रा मुझे बताइये।
Please listen. (Pardon me)	***zarā suniye.*** ज़रा सुनिये।
Please give me this.	***zarā mujhe yeh dījiye.*** ज़रा मुझे यह दीजिये।
Please give me that.	***zarā mujhe voh dījiye.*** ज़रा मुझे वह दीजिये।
Please take this from me.	***zarā yeh mujh se lījiye.*** ज़रा यह मुझसे लीजिये।
Please pay attention. (give a little attention)	***zarā dhyān dījiye.*** ज़रा ध्यान दीजिये।

3.3 Starting a conversation

May I say something?	***maĩ kuch kahū̃?*** मैं कुछ कहूँ?

May I ask something?	***maĩ kuch pūchū̃?*** मैं कुछ पूछूँ?
May I help you?	***maĩ āpkī madad karū̃?*** मैं आपकी मदद करूँ?
May I sit here?	***maĩ yahā̃ baiṭhū̃?*** मैं यहाँ बैठूँ?
May I see (this)?	***maĩ zarā (ise) dekhū̃?*** मैं ज़रा (इसे) देखूँ?
May I take (this)?	***maĩ zarā (ise) lū̃?*** मैं ज़रा (इसे) लूँ?
May I give this (to you)?	***kyā maĩ (āpko) yeh dū̃?*** क्या मैं (आपको) यह दूँ?
May I take this (from you)?	***kyā maĩ (āpse) yeh lū̃?*** क्या मैं (आपसे) यह लूँ?
May I listen?	***maĩ sunū̃?*** मैं सुनूँ?
May I watch?	***maĩ dekhū̃?*** मैं देखूँ?
May I come?	***maĩ āū̃?*** मैं आऊँ?
May I go?	***maĩ jāū̃?*** मैं जाऊँ?
Will you help me? (m/f) (polite)	***kyā āp merī madad karẽge/karẽgī?*** क्या आप मेरी मदद करेंगे/करेंगी?
Will you come with me? (m/f) (polite)	***kyā āp mere sāth āẽge/āẽgī?*** क्या आप मेरे साथ आएँगे/आएँगी?
Will you come with me? (m/f) (informal)	***kyā tum mere sāth āoge/āogī?*** क्या तुम मेरे साथ आओगे/आओगी?
Would you take our photo? (m/f) (polite)	***kyā āp hamārī foṭo khĩcẽge/khĩcẽgī?*** क्या आप हमारी फ़ोटो खींचेंगे/खींचेंगी?

Would you take my photo? (m/f) (polite)	***kyā āp merī foṭo khī̃cẽge/khī̃cẽgī?*** क्या आप मेरी फ़ोटो खींचेंगे/खींचेंगी?
Please don't bother me.	***mujhe tang mat kījiye.*** मुझे तंग मत कीजिये।
Please don't bother us.	***hamẽ tang mat kījiye.*** हमें तंग मत कीजिये।
Please don't bother them/ him/her. (close) (polite)	***inhẽ tang mat kījiye.*** इन्हें तंग मत कीजिये।
Please don't bother them/ him/her. (far) (polite)	***unhẽ tang mat kījiye.*** उन्हें तंग मत कीजिये।
Please don't bother him/her. (close) (polite)	***ise tang mat kījiye.*** इसे तंग मत कीजिये।
Please don't bother him/her. (far) (polite)	***use tang mat kījiye.*** उसे तंग मत कीजिये।
Please go. (polite)	***jāiye.*** जाइये।
Go. (informal)	***jāo.*** जाओ।
Go/Scram! (intimate/impolite)	***jā!*** जा!

3.4 A chat about the weather

It is really hot/cold today. (much heat/cold is happening)	***āj bahut garmī/ṭhaṇd ho rahī hai.*** आज बहुत गर्मी/ठंड हो रही है।
It was really hot/cold yesterday. (much heat/cold was happening)	***kal bahut garmī/ṭhaṇd ho rahī thī.*** कल बहुत गर्मी/ठंड हो रही थी।
I feel very hot/cold.	***mujhe bahut garmī/ṭhaṇḍ lag rahī hai.*** मुझे बहुत गर्मी/ठंड लग रही है।

I was feeling very hot/cold yesterday.	***kal mujhe bahut garmī/ṭhaṇḍ lag rahī thī.*** कल मुझे बहुत गर्मी/ठंड लग रही थी।
Today's weather is beautiful (pleasing).	***āj kā mausam suhāvnā hai.*** आज का मौसम सुहावना है।
Yesterday's weather was beautiful (pleasing).	***kal kā mausam suhāvnā thā.*** कल का मौसम सुहावना था।
Today's weather is very bad.	***āj kā mausam bahut kharāb hai.*** आज का मौसम बहुत ख़राब है।
Yesterday's weather was bad.	***kal kā mausam bahut kharāb thā.*** कल का मौसम बहुत ख़राब था।
It is windy today. (much wind is moving)	***āj bahut havā cal rahī hai.*** आज बहुत हवा चल रही है।
The fog is bad today. (today there is much fog)	***āj bahut kuhrā hai.*** आज बहुत कुहरा है।
The pollution is bad today.	***āj pradūṣaṇ bahut zyādā hai.*** आज प्रदूषण बहुत ज़्यादा है।

3.5 Hobbies

āpko kin cizõ kā śauq hai? आपको किन चीज़ों का शौक़ है?	What are your hobbies? (polite) (to you what hobbies are)
mujhe film dekhne kā śauq hai. मुझे फ़िल्म देखने का शौक़ है।	I like watching films. (to me the hobby of watching films is)
kyā tumhẽ film dekhnā acchā lagtā hai? क्या तुम्हें फ़िल्म देखना अच्छा लगता है?	Do you like watching films? (informal)

mujhe film dekhnā bahut acchā lagtā hai. मुझे फ़िल्म देखना बहुत अच्छा लगता है।	I really like watching films.

I like reading books.	***mujhe kitāb paṛhnā acchā lagtā hai.*** मुझे किताब पढ़ना अच्छा लगता है।
I like listening to music.	***mujhe sangīt sunnā acchā lagtā hai.*** मुझे संगीत सुनना अच्छा लगता है।
I like cooking.	***mujhe khānā pakānā acchā lagtā hai.*** मुझे खाना पकाना अच्छा लगता है।
I like traveling. (wandering)	***mujhe ghūmnā acchā lagtā hai.*** मुझे घूमना अच्छा लगता है।

3.6 Invitations

What will you do this evening? (m/f)(polite)	***āj śām ko āp kyā karẽge/karẽgī?*** आज शाम को आप क्या करेंगे/करेंगी?
What will you do this evening? (m/f)(informal)	***āj śām ko tum kyā karoge/karogī?*** आज शाम को तुम क्या करोगे/करोगी?
What are you about to do this evening? (m/f) (polite)	***āj śām ko āp kyā karnevāle/karnevālī haĩ?*** आज शाम को आप क्या करनेवाले/करनेवाली हैं?
What are you about to do this evening? (m/f) (informal)	***āj śām ko tum kyā karnevāle/karnevālī ho?*** आज शाम को तुम क्या करनेवाले/करनेवाली हो?
Are you about to do something this evening? (m/f) (polite)	***kyā āj śām ko āp kuch karnevāle/karnevālī haĩ?*** क्या आज शाम को आप कुछ करनेवाले/करनेवाली हैं?

Are you about to do something this evening? (m/f) (informal)	***kyā āj śām ko tum kuch karnevāle/ karnevālī ho?*** क्या आज शाम को तुम कुछ करनेवाले/करनेवाली हो?
What are you doing right now? (m/f)(polite)	***abhī āp kyā kar rahe haĩ/kar rahī haĩ?*** अभी आप क्या कर रहे हैं/कर रही हैं?
What are you doing right now? (m/f)(informal)	***abhī tum kyā kar rahe ho/kar rahī ho?*** अभी तुम क्या कर रहे हो/कर रही हो?
Will you come to my home tonight? (m/f) (polite)	***kyā āp āj rāt ko mere ghar āẽge/āẽgī?*** क्या आप आज रात को मेरे घर आएँगे/आएँगी?
Will you come to my home tonight? (m/f) (informal)	***kyā tum aj rat ko mere ghar āoge/āogī?*** क्या तुम आज रात को मेरे घर आओगे/आओगी?
Will you drink tea with me? (m/f) (polite)	***kyā āp mere sāth cāy piẽge/piẽgī?*** क्या आप मेरे साथ चाय पिएँगे/पिएँगी?
Will you drink tea with me? (m/f) (informal)	***kyā tum mere sāth cāy piyoge/piyogī?*** क्या तुम मेरे साथ चाय पियोगे/पियोगी?
Will you eat with us? (m/f) (polite)	***kyā āp hamāre sāth khāẽge/khāẽgī?*** क्या आप हमारे साथ खाएँगे/खाएँगी?
Will you eat with us? (m/f) (informal)	***kyā tum hamāre sāth khāoge/khāogī?*** क्या तुम हमारे साथ खाओगे/खाओगी?
Will you go to see a film with me? (m/f) (informal)	***mere sāth film dekhne caloge/calogī?*** मेरे साथ फ़िल्म देखने चलोगे/चलोगी?
Will you come shopping with me? (m/f) (informal)	***mere sāth śāpiṅg karne caloge/calogī?*** मेरे साथ शॉपिंग करने चलोगे/चलोगी?

Will you have dinner (food) with me? (m/f) (informal)	***mere sāth khānā khāne caloge/calogī?*** मेरे साथ खाना खाने चलोगे/चलोगी?
Will you go for a stroll with me? (m/f) (informal)	***mere sāth ṭehalne caloge/calogī?*** मेरे साथ टहलने चलोगे/चलोगी?
Certainly! I would love to. (much happiness will occur)	***zarūr! bahut khuśī hogī.*** ज़रूर! बहुत ख़ुशी होगी।
Certainly. That will be fun. (much enjoyment will come)	***zarūr! bahut mazā āegā.*** ज़रूर! बहुत मज़ा आएगा।
This is really enjoyable.	***yeh bahut mazedār hai.*** यह बहुत मज़ेदार है।
I will not be able to come. (m/f)	***maĩ ā nahī̃ pāū̃gā/pāū̃gī.*** मैं आ नहीं पाऊँगा/पाऊँगी।
Please forgive me.	***māf kījiye.*** माफ़ कीजिये।
I really want to come. (mf)	***maĩ sacmuc ānā cāhtā/cāhtī hū̃.*** मैं सचमुच आना चाहता/चाहती हूँ।
I really want to come. (much coming's mind/heart is)	***āne kā bahut man hai.*** आने का बहुत मन है।
I don't have time.	***mere pās samay/ṭāim nahī̃ hai.*** मेरे पास समय/टाइम नहीं है।
Perhaps tomorrow.	***śāyad kal.*** शायद कल।
I have to work.	***mujhe kām karnā hai.*** मुझे काम करना है।
I will come tomorrow. (m/f)	***maĩ kal āū̃gā/āū̃gī.*** मैं कल आऊँगा/आऊँगी।
We will meet in the evening.	***ham śām ko milẽge.*** हम शाम को मिलेंगे।

I will meet you tomorrow. (mf/) (polite)	***maĩ kal āp se milū̃gā/milū̃gī.*** मैं कल आपसे मिलूँगा/मिलूँगी।
I will meet you tomorrow. (mf/) (informal)	***maĩ kal tum se milū̃gā/milū̃gī.*** मैं कल तुमसे मिलूँगा/मिलूँगी।

3.7 Paying compliments

You are very beautiful/ handsome. (polite)	***āp bahut sundar haĩ.*** आप बहुत सुंदर हैं।
You are very beautiful/ handsome. (informal)	***tum bahut sundar ho.*** तुम बहुत सुंदर हो।
Your clothes are very beautiful. (polite)	***āpke kapṛe bahut sundar haĩ.*** आपके कपड़े बहुत सुंदर हैं।
Your home is very beautiful. (polite)	***āpkā ghar bahut sundar hai.*** आपका घर बहुत सुंदर है।
This food is delicious (tasty).	***yeh khānā bahut lazīz/svādiṣṭ hai.*** यह खाना बहुत लज़ीज़/स्वादिष्ट है।
This food is very enjoyable.	***yeh khānā bahut mazedār hai.*** यह खाना बहुत मज़ेदार है।
I really enjoyed the food.	***khānā bahut pasand āyā.*** खाना बहुत पसंद आया।
I really enjoyed this film.	***yeh film bahut pasand āyī.*** यह फ़िल्म बहुत पसंद आयी।
What a good boy.	***kitnā acchā laṛkā hai.*** कितना अच्छा लड़का है।
What a good girl.	***kitnī acchī laṛkī hai.*** कितनी अच्छी लड़की है।
You are very nice. (informal)	***tum bahut acche/acchī ho.*** तुम बहुत अच्छे/अच्छी हो।

3.8 Intimate comments/questions

I like being with you. (informal)	***tumhāre sāth mujhe bahut acchā lagtā hai.*** तुम्हारे साथ मुझे बहुत अच्छा लगता है।
I miss you a lot. (polite)	***āpkī bahut yād ātī hai.*** आपकी बहुत याद आती है।
I miss you a lot. (informal)	***tumhārī bahut yād ātī hai.*** तुम्हारी बहुत याद आती है।
I care for you. (polite) (your much concern/care is)	***āpkī bahut parvāh hai.*** आपकी बहुत परवाह है।
I care for you. (informal) (your much concern/care is)	***tumhārī bahut parvāh hai.*** तुम्हारी बहुत परवाह है।
Take care of yourself. (polite) (keep your thought)	***apnā <u>kh</u>yāl rakhiye.*** अपना ख़्याल रखिये।
Take care of yourself. (informal) (keep your thought)	***apnā <u>kh</u>yāl rakho.*** अपना ख़्याल रखो।
I am worried about you. (polite) (your much concern is happening)	***āpkī bahut fikr ho rahī hai.*** आपकी बहुत फ़िक्र हो रही है।
Your smile is beautiful. (informal)	***tumhārī muskān bahut sundar hai.*** तुम्हारी मुस्कान बहुत सुंदर है।
You have beautiful eyes. (informal)	***tumhārī ā̃khẽ bahut sundar haĩ.*** तुम्हारी आँखें बहुत सुंदर हैं।
I like you a lot. (m) (informal)	***tum mujhe bahut acche lagte ho.*** तुम मुझे बहुत अच्छे लगते हो।
I like you a lot. (f) (informal)	***tum mujhe bahut acchī lagtī ho.*** तुम मुझे बहुत अच्छी लगती हो।

I love you. (informal) (from you love has happened)	***tumse pyār ho gayā hai.*** तुमसे प्यार हो गया है।
I too. (informal) (to me also)	***mujhe bhī.*** मुझे भी।
I love you. (m/f) (informal)	***maĩ tumse pyār kartā/kartī hū̃.*** मैं तुमसे प्यार करता/करती हूँ।
I too. (informal) (I also)	***maĩ bhī.*** मैं भी।

3.9 Congratulations and condolences

Congratulations!	***badhāī/mubārak ho!*** बधाई/मुबारक हो!
Happy birthday!	***janmdin mubārak ho!*** जन्मदिन मुबारक हो!
I am sorry to hear this. (having heard sorrow happened)	***sunkar bahut afsos huā.*** सुनकर बहुत अफ़सोस हुआ।
This is very sad. (a matter of much sadness)	***yeh bahut dukh kī bāt hai.*** यह बहुत दुख की बात है।
This is a very happy thing.	***yeh bahut khuśī kī bāt hai.*** यह बहुत ख़ुशी की बात है।
Happy Eid!	***īd mubārak ho!*** ईद मुबारक हो!
Happy Holi!	***holī mubārak ho!*** होली मुबारक हो!
Happy Divali!	***divālī mubārak ho!*** दिवाली मुबारक हो!
Happy New Year!	***nayā sāl mubārak ho!*** नया साल मुबारक हो!

Hand out the sweets. (make the mouth sweet)	***mũh mīṭhā karo.*** मुँह मीठा करो।

3.10 Arrangements

When will we meet again?	***ham phir kab milẽge?*** हम फिर कब मिलेंगे?
Where shall we meet?	***ham kahã̄ milẽge?*** हम कहाँ मिलेंगे?
When shall we meet?	***ham kab milẽge?*** हम कब मिलेंगे?
What time shall we meet?	***ham kitne baje milẽge?*** हम कितने बजे मिलेंगे?
What do you want to do? (m/f) (polite)	***āp kyā karnā cāhte/cāhtī haĩ?*** आप क्या करना चाहते/चाहती हैं?
Shall we go to see a film?	***film dekhne calẽge?*** फ़िल्म देखने चलेंगे?
Shall we go to eat (food)?	***khānā khāne calẽge?*** खाना खाने चलेंगे?

3.11 Being the host(ess)

andar āiye. अंदर आइये।	Please come inside.
kyā āp cāy yā kāfī lẽge/lẽgī? क्या आप चाय या कॉफ़ी लेंगे/लेंगी?	Will you have tea or coffee? (m/f) (polite)
kyā tum cāy yā kāfī loge/logī? क्या तुम चाय या कॉफ़ी लोगे/लोगी?	Will you have tea or coffee? (m/f) (informal)

I have just had tea. (m/f) (I have come having drunk tea)	***cāy pī kar āyā/āyī hū̃.*** चाय पीकर आया/आयी हूँ।
Have dinner with us. (polite) (having eaten food, please go)	***khānā khā kar jāiye.*** खाना खा कर जाइये।
I have already eaten. (m/f) (I have come having eaten)	***khānā khā kar āyā/āyī hū̃.*** खाना खाकर आया/आयी हूँ।
Will you have (take) alcohol? (m/f) (polite)	***āp śarāb lẽge/lẽgī?*** आप शराब लेंगे/लेंगी?
Will you have (take) beer? (m/f) (polite)	***āp biyar lẽge/lẽgī?*** आप बियर लेंगे/लेंगी?
Will you have (take) whiskey? (m/f) (polite)	***āp whiskī lẽge/lẽgī?*** आप ह्विस्की लेंगे/लेंगी?
Please take some more.	***kuch aur lījiye.*** कुछ और लीजिये।
Please eat some more.	***kuch aur khāiye.*** कुछ और खाइये।

3.12 Saying goodbye

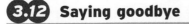

Goodbye	***namaste/namskār*** नमस्ते/नमस्कार
I will write to you. (m/f) (polite)	***maĩ āpko likhū̃gā/likhū̃gī.*** मैं आपको लिखूँगा/लिखूँगी।
I will write to you. (m/f) (informal)	***maĩ tumko likhū̃gā/likhū̃gī.*** मैं तुमको लिखूँगा/लिखूँगी।
I will phone you when I get there. (having gone there I will call)	***vahā̃ jā kar maĩ fon karū̃gā/karū̃gī.*** वहाँ जाकर मैं फ़ोन करूँगा/करूँगी।
Will you phone me? (m/f) (polite)	***āp mujhe fon karẽge/karẽgī?*** आप मुझे फ़ोन करेंगे/करेंगी?

I really enjoyed it here. (to me much enjoyment came)	***mujhe yahā̃ bahut mazā āyā.*** मुझे यहाँ बहुत मज़ा आया।
Thank you very much.	***bahut bahut śukriyā.*** बहुत बहुत शुक्रिया।
I hope that we meet again. (to me the hope is that…)	***mujhe ummīd hai ki ham phir milẽge.*** मुझे उम्मीद है कि हम फिर मिलेंगे।
Good luck.	***śubhkāmnāẽ*** शुभकामनाएँ
Best wishes.	***śubhkāmnāẽ*** शुभकामनाएँ
Have a good (auspicious) trip.	***śubh yātrā.*** शुभ यात्रा।
When will you return? (m/f) (polite)	***āp kab vāpas āẽge/āẽgī?*** आप कब वापस आएँगे/आएँगी?
When will you come back? (m/f) (informal)	***tum kab vāpas āoge/āogī?*** तुम कब वापस आओगे/आओगी?
Please write when you get there. (polite) (having gone there please write a letter)	***vahā̃ jā kar patra likhiye.*** वहाँ जाकर पत्र लिखिये।
Please write when you get there. (informal) (having gone there please write a letter)	***vahā̃ jā kar patra likknā.*** वहाँ जाकर पत्र लिखना।
Please phone when you get there. (polite) (having gone there please phone)	***vahā̃ jā kar fon kījiye.*** वहाँ जाकर फ़ोन कीजिये।
Please phone when you get there. (informal) (having gone there please phone)	***vahā̃ jā kar fon karnā.*** वहाँ जाकर फ़ोन करना।

I will wait for you. (m/f) (polite)	***maĩ āpkā intazār karū̃gā/karū̃gī.*** मैं आपका इंतज़ार करूँगा/करूँगी।
I will wait for you. (m/f) (informal)	***maĩ tumhārā intazār karū̃gā/karū̃gī.*** मैं तुम्हारा इंतज़ार करूँगा/करूँगी।
Please take my address. (polite)	***merā patā lījiye.*** मेरा पता लीजिये।
Please take my address. (informal)	***merā patā lo.*** मेरा पता लो।

4 Eating Out

4. Eating Out

4.1 At the restaurant

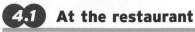

Is this pure vegetarian?	***kyā yeh śudh śākāhārī hai?*** क्या यह शुद्ध शाकाहारी है?
I eat meat. (m/f)	***maĩ māns khātā/khātī hū̃.*** मैं मांस खाता/खाती हूँ।
I do not eat meat. (m/f)	***maĩ māns nahī̃ khātā/khātī.*** मैं मांस नहीं खाता/खाती।
I drink alcohol. (m/f)	***maĩ śarāb pītā/pītī hū̃.*** मैं शराब पीता/पीती हूँ।
I do not drink alcohol. (m/f)	***maĩ śarāb nahī̃ pītā/pītī.*** मैं शराब नहीं पीता/पीती।
I used to eat meat. (m/f)	***maĩ māns khātā thā/khātī thī.*** मैं मांस खाता था/खाती थी।
I used to drink alcohol. (m/f)	***maĩ śarāb pītā thā/pītī thī.*** मैं शराब पीता था/पीती थी।
I am (not) a vegetarian.	***maĩ śākāhārī (nahī̃) hū̃.*** मैं शाकाहारी (नहीं) हूँ।
I used to be a vegetarian. (m/f)	***maĩ śākāhārī thā/thī.*** मैं शाकाहारी था/थी।
Is the food very spicy?	***kyā yahā̃ kā khānā bahut masāledār hai?*** क्या यहाँ का खाना बहुत मसालेदार है?
We cannot eat very spicy food.	***ham bahut masāledār khānā khā nahī̃ sakte.*** हम बहुत मसालेदार खाना खा नहीं सकते।
Is your restaurant open?	***kyā āpkā resṭrā̃ is samay khulā hai?*** क्या आपका रेस्ट्राँ इस समय खुला है?

May we sit here?	***kyā ham yahā̃ baiṭhẽ?*** क्या हम यहाँ बैठें?
May I see a menu?	***kyā maĩ menū kārḍ dekhū̃*** क्या मैं मेनू कार्ड देखूँ?
Could you bring one more chair? (m/f)	***āp ek aur kursī lāẽge/lāẽgī?*** आप एक और कुरसी लाएँगे?
Could you please clean the table. (m/f)	***āp mez sāf karẽge/karẽgī?*** आप मेज़ साफ़ करेंगे?

pīne ke liye kyā milegā? पीने के लिये क्या मिलेगा?	What is available to drink? (what will be found for drinking)
kyā cāy milegī? क्या चाय मिलेगी?	Do you have tea? (will tea be available)
kyā lassī milegī? क्या लस्सी मिलेगी?	Do you have lassi? (will lassi be available)
kyā samose milẽge? क्या समोसे मिलेंगे?	Do you have samosas? (will samosas be available)

Please don't put ice in it.	***us mẽ barf mat ḍāliye.*** उसमें बर्फ़ मत डालिये।
Please put ice in it.	***us mẽ barf ḍāliye.*** उसमें बर्फ़ डालिये।
I do not want/need ice.	***mujhe barf nahī̃ cāhiye.*** मुझे बर्फ़ नहीं चाहिये।
Is the water boiled?	***kyā pānī ublā huā hai?*** क्या पानी उबला हुआ है?
Is the water filtered?	***kyā pānī filṭarḍ hai?*** क्या पानी फ़िल्टर्ड है?
I like spicy food.	***mujhe masāledār khānā pasand hai.*** मुझे मसालेदार खाना पसंद है।

I don't like spicy food. — ***mujhe masāledār khānā pasand nahī̃ hai.***
मुझे मसालेदार खाना पसंद नहीं है।

I really like roti (bread). — ***mujhe roṭī bahut pasand hai.***
मुझे रोटी बहुत पसंद है।

4.2 Ordering

Sir! — ***bhāī sāhab!***
भाई साहब!

Pardon me (please listen). — ***suniye.***
सुनिये।

We would like to order. — ***ham ārḍar denā cāhte haĩ.***
हम ऑर्डर देना चाहते हैं।

What do you want/need? (polite) — ***āpko kyā cāhiye?***
आपको क्या चाहिये?

What do you want/need? (informal) — ***tumko kyā cāhiye?***
तुमको क्या चाहिये?

Please bring some water. — ***zarā pānī lāiye.***
ज़रा पानी लाइये।

Please take our order. — ***hamārā ārḍar lījiye.***
हमारा ऑर्डर लीजिये।

Please bring a (one) dal (lentil dish). — ***ek dāl lāiye***
एक दाल लाइये।

Please bring some more sambhar. — ***kuch aur sā̃bhar lāiye.***
कुछ और साँभर लाइये।

Please bring some more chutney. — ***kuch aur caṭnī lāiye.***
कुछ और चटनी लाइये।

Please bring some more pickle. — ***kuch aur acār lāiye.***
कुछ और अचार लाइये।

Please bring some salt. — ***namak lāiye.***
नमक लाइये।

We will have (take) rice.	***ham cāval lẽge.***	हम चावल लेंगे।
We will eat rice.	***ham cāval khāẽge.***	हम चावल खाएँगे।
He/She will have (take) roti.	***ye roṭī lẽge/lẽgī.***	ये रोटी लेंगे/लेंगी।
What will you have (take)? (m/f) (polite)	***āp kyā lẽge/lẽgī?***	आप क्या लेंगे/लेंगी?
What will you have (take)? (m/f) (informal)	***tum kyā loge/logī?***	तुम क्या लोगे/लोगी?
What would you like? (m/f) (what will you choose)	***āp kyā pasand karẽge/karẽgī?***	आप क्या पसंद करेंगे/करेंगी?
I will eat biriyani. (m/f)	***maĩ biryānī khāū̃gā/khāū̃gī.***	मैं बिरयानी खाऊँगा/खाऊँगी।
Please give us five more minutes.	***hamẽ pā̃c minaṭ aur dījiye.***	हमें पाँच मिनट और दीजिये।
Please bring the food quickly.	***khānā jaldī lāiye.***	खाना जल्दी लाइये।
Please bring tea.	***cāy lāiye.***	चाय लाइये।

4.3 The bill

Please bring the bill.	***bil lāiye.***	बिल लाइये।
This is not our bill.	***yeh hamārā bil nahī̃ hai.***	यह हमारा बिल नहीं है।
This does not seem right.	***yeh ṭhīk nahī̃ lagtā.***	यह ठीक नहीं लगता।
Please take the money.	***paise lījiye.***	पैसे लीजिये।

We did not get the …. (m/f) (…was not received)	***… nahī̃ milā/milī.*** … नहीं मिला/मिली।

4.4 Complaints

It has been a long time. (much delay has attached)	***bahut der lagī (hai).*** बहुत देर लगी (है)।
Will it take much longer? (will much delay attach)	***bahut der lagegī?*** बहुत देर लगेगी?
How long will it take? (how much delay will attach)	***kitnī der lagegī?*** कितनी देर लगेगी?
It is taking a long time. (how much delay will attach)	***bahut der lag rahī hai.*** बहुत देर लग रही है।
This is cold. (m/f)	***yeh ṭhaṇḍā/ṭhaṇḍī hai*** यह ठंडा/ठंडी है।
This is too (much) spicy.	***yeh bahut zyādā masāledār hai.*** यह बहुत ज़्यादा मसालेदार है।
This is not mine.	***yeh merā nahī̃ hai.*** यह मेरा नहीं है।
This is not ours.	***yeh hamārā nahī̃ hai.*** यह हमारा नहीं है।
This is not yours. (polite)	***yeh āpkā nahī̃ hai.*** यह आपका नहीं है।
This is not yours. (informal)	***yeh tumhārā nahī̃ hai.*** यह तुम्हारा नहीं है।
This is not his/hers. (close) (polite)	***yeh inkā nahī̃ hai.*** यह इनका नहीं है।
This is not his/hers. (close) (informal)	***yeh iskā nahī̃ hai.*** यह इसका नहीं है।
This is not his/hers. (far) (polite)	***yeh unkā nahī̃ hai.*** यह उनका नहीं है।

This is not his/hers. (far) (informal)	***yeh uskā nahī̃ hai.*** यह उसका नहीं है।
I cannot eat this. (m/f)	***maĩ yeh khā nahī̃ saktā/saktī.*** मैं यह खा नहीं सकता/सकती।
There is too much salt in this.	***is mẽ bahut zyādā namak hai.*** इस में बहुत ज़्यादा नमक है।
There is not enough salt in this.	***is mẽ kam namak hai.*** इस में कम नमक है।
This is not fresh.	***yeh tāzā nahī̃ hai.*** यह ताज़ा नहीं है।
This is not hot.	***yeh garm nahī̃ hai.*** यह गर्म नहीं है।
This is not hot enough.	***yeh bilkul bhī garm nahī̃ hai.*** यह बिल्कुल भी गर्म नहीं है।
This is too hot.	***yeh zyādā garm hai.*** यह ज़्यादा गर्म है।
This is stale.	***yeh bāsī hai.*** यह बासी है।
This is not clean.	***yeh sāf nahī̃ hai.*** यह साफ़ नहीं है।

4.5 Paying a compliment

The food was very tasty.	***khānā bahut lazīz/svādiṣṭ thā.*** खाना बहुत लज़ीज़/स्वादिष्ट था।
The food was excellent.	***khānā bahut baṛhiyā thā.*** खाना बहुत बढ़िया था।
I really liked the lentils. (f)	***dāl bahut pasand āyī.*** दाल बहुत पसंद आयी।
I really liked the vegetable dish. (f)	***sabzī bahut pasand āyī.*** सब्ज़ी बहुत पसंद आयी।

I really liked the rice. (m)	***cāval bahut pasand āyā.*** चावल बहुत पसंद आया।
I really liked the samosas. (m, pl)	***samose bahut pasand āye.*** समोसे बहुत पसंद आये।

4.6 The menu

In the Beginning ***śurū mẽ*** शुरू में	Drinks (for drinking) ***pīne ke liye*** पीने के लिये	Vegetable(s) (f) ***sabzī*** सब्ज़ी
From the Garden ***baghīce se*** बग़ीचे से	Sweets ***mīṭhā*** मीठा	Fish (f) ***machlī*** मछली
Meat (m) ***gośt/māns*** गोश्त/मांस		

4.7 Alphabetical list of dishes and drinks

alcohol (f)
śarāb
शराब

barfi (a sweetmeat made from milk) (f)
barfī
बर्फ़ी

beef (m)
gāy kā gośt/māns
गाय का गोश्त/मांस

bhatura (bread baked on a griddle and deep fried) (m)
bhaṭūrā
भटूरा

biriyani (f)
biryānī
बिरयानी

bread (f)
roṭī/capātī
रोटी/चपाती

butter (m)
makkhan
मक्खन

buttermilk (f)
chāch
छाछ

cabbage (f)
band gobhī
बंद गोभी

carrot halva (halva with carrots) (m)
gājar kā halvā
गाजर का हलवा

cauliflower (f)
phūl gobhī
फूल गोभी

cauliflower dish (f)
gobhī kī sabzī
गोभी की सब्ज़ी

chat (spicy fast food) (f)
cāṭ
चाट

cheese (m)
panīr
पनीर

chicken (m)
murgh
मुर्ग़

chickpeas (m, pl)
chole
छोले

chickpeas and bhatura (spicy chickpeas with fried bread) (m)
chole bhaṭūre
छोले भटूरे

chutney (f)
caṭnī
चटनी

dosa (m)
ḍosā
डोसा

eggplant (m)
baĩgan
बैंगन

eggplant dish (m)
baĩgan bhartā
बैंगन भरता

fish (f)
machlī
मछली

fruit (m)
phal
फल

(fruit) juice (m)
(phalõ kā) ras/jūs
(फलों का) रस/जूस

fruit raita (m)
phalõ kā rāytā
फलों का रायता

garlic (m)
lehsun
लहसुन

ghee (clarifed butter) (m)
ghī
घी

goat's meat (m)
bakre kā gośt/māns
बकरे का गोश्त/मांस

gourd (f)
laukī
लौकी

gourd vegetable dish (f)
laukī kī sabzī
लौकी की सब्ज़ी

green beans (m)
bīns
बीन्स

gulab jamun (fried sweet made from milk, served hot in syrup) (m)
gulāb jāmun
गुलाब जामुन

halva (sweet dish made from lentils, semolina, or rice and sugar) (m)
halvā
हलवा

jalebi (fried crisp sweet in syrup) (f)
jalebī
जलेबी

khoya (solidified milk, the base of most sweets made of milk) (m)
khoyā
खोया

kidney beans (m)
rājmā
राजमा

kulfi (Indian ice cream) (f)
qulfī
कुलफ़ी

laddu (sweet made from chickpea flour) (m)
laḍḍū
लड्डू

lassi (cold, sweet yoghurt drink) (f)
lassī
लस्सी

lentils (f)
dāl
दाल

lentils and rice (m)
dāl cāval
दाल चावल

meat (m)
gośt/māns
गोश्त/मांस

mutton (m)
bheṛ kā gośt/māns
भेड़ का गोश्त/मांस

nan (baked bread, plain flour) (f)
nān
नान

onion (m)
pyāz
प्याज़

orange juice (sweet lime) (m)
mausamī kā ras
मौसमी का रस

paratha (fried bread, unleaved wheat flour) (m)
parā̃ṭhā
पराँठा

peas (f)
maṭar
मटर

peas and cheese (m)
maṭar panīr
मटर पनीर

pickle (m)
acār
अचार

potato (m)
ālū
आलू

potato and cauliflower dish (f)
ālū gobhī
आलू गोभी

potatoes and peas (f)
ālū maṭar
आलू मटर

potato paratha (m)
ālū parā̃ṭhā
आलू पराँठा

pumpkin (m)
kaddū
कद्दू

puri (fried bread)
pūṛī
पूड़ी

rasmalai (sweet dish, made of cream, milk and syrup) (f)
rasmalāī
रसमलाई

rice (m)
cāval
चावल

rice pudding (f)
khīr
खीर

roti (unleavened bread baked) (f)
roṭī
रोटी

sambhar (soupy dish made out of lentils and vegetables served with dosa) (m)
sā̃bhar
साँभर

soda (m)
soḍā
सोडा

spinach (m)
pālak
पालक

spinach and cheese dish (m)
pālak panīr
पालक पनीर

vegetable (f/m)
sabzī/sāg
सब्ज़ी/साग

yoghurt (m)
dahī
दही

chicken (m)
murgh
मुर्ग़

4.8 Well-known dishes

tandur (a clay oven) (m)	***tandūr***	तंदूर
tava (iron griddle) (m)	***tavā***	तवा

mung dal (f) (a typical yellow lentil dish)	***mũg kī dāl*** मूँग की दाल
arhar dal (f) (a yellow-brown lentil dish)	***arhar kī dāl*** अरहर की दाल
pulav (m) (rice fried in ghee and cooked with cumin and stock)	***pulāv*** पुलाव
kabab (m) (barbequed mutton cooked on skewers)	***kabāb*** कबाब
korma (m) (a rich brown curry with chicken, mutton or vegetables)	***qormā*** क़ोरमा
kofta (m) (minced balls of meat or vegetables served in a sauce)	***koftā*** कोफ़्ता
tandoori chicken (m)	***tandūrī cikan*** तंदूरी चिकन
okra (f)	***bhiṇḍī*** भिंडी
dosa (m) (a pancake made from rice flour)	***ḍosā*** डोसा
pakora (m) (fried batter of gram flour with vegetables)	***pakauṛā*** पकौड़ा

5 Getting Around

5. Getting Around

5.1 Asking directions

May I ask you something?	***maĩ āp se kuch pūchū̃*** मैं आपसे कुछ पूछूँ?
I have lost my way (path). (m/f)	***maĩ rāstā bhūl gayā/gayī.*** मैं रास्ता भूल गया/गयी।
Where is the ...?	***... kahā̃ hai?*** ... कहाँ है?
Is the ... ahead?	***kyā ... āge hai?*** क्या ... आगे है?
How far is the ... from here?	***... yahā̃ se kitnī dūr hai?*** ... यहाँ से कितनी दूर है?
Is the ... close to here?	***kyā ... yahā̃ se nazdīk hai?*** क्या ... यहाँ से नज़दीक है?
Could you show me on the map? (m/f)	***āp naqśe par dikhāẽge/dikhāẽgī?*** आप नक़्शे पर दिखाएँगे/दिखाएँगी?
Go straight (polite)	***sīdhe jāiye.*** सीधे जाइये।
Turn left ahead. (polite) (having gone ahead, turn left)	***āge jākar bāyī̃ taraf muṛiye.*** आगे जाकर बायीं तरफ़ मुड़िये।
Turn right ahead. (polite) (having gone ahead, turn left)	***āge jākar dāhinī taraf muṛiye.*** आगे जाकर दाहिनी तरफ़ मुड़िये।

street (f) ***saṛak*** सड़क	flyover (m) ***flāī-ovar*** फ़्लाइ-ओवर	laneway (f) ***galī*** गली
way (m) (path) ***rāstā*** रास्ता	bridge (m) ***pul*** पुल	at the intersection ***caurāhe par*** चौराहे पर

road (m) ***mārg*** मार्ग	at the corner ***kone par*** कोने पर	traffic light (f) ***battī*** बत्ती

5.2 Traffic signs

Stop ***ṭhehriye*** ठहरिये	Intersection ahead ***āge caurāhā hai.*** आगे चौराहा है।	Drive carefully (remain vigilant) ***sāvadhān rahẽ*** सावधान रहें
Traffic signal ahead ***āge battī hai*** आगे बत्ती है।	There is a bend ahead. ***āge moṛ hai.*** आगे मोड़ है।	Road closed ***rāstā band hai.*** रास्ता बंद है।
Drive slowly ***dhīre calẽ*** धीरे चलें	Incline/slope (f) ***ḍhalān*** ढलान	Sharp bend (m) ***tīvra moṛ*** तीव्र मोड़

5.3 Cars, bicycles/mopeds

battery (f) (car) ***baiṭrī*** बैट्री	engine (m) ***injan*** इंजन	accelerator (m) ***ekselareṭar*** एक्सेलरेटर
light (f) ***battī*** बत्ती	windshield (m) ***śiśā*** शीशा	gear (m) ***giyar*** गियर
mirror (m) ***āinā*** आइना	break (m) ***brek*** ब्रेक	radiator (m) ***reḍiyeṭar*** रेडियेटर
door (m) ***darvāzā*** दरवाज़ा	pedal (m) ***paiḍal*** पैडल	low beam (m) ***ḍipar*** डिपर
trunk (f) ***ḍikkī*** डिक्की	chain (f) ***zanjīr*** ज़ंजीर	steering wheel (m) ***cakkā*** चक्का

muffler (m)	window (f)	clutch (m)
maflar	***khiṛkī***	***klac***
मफ़लर	खिड़की	क्लच

5.4 The gas station

peṭrol bhar dījiye. पेट्रोल भर दीजिये।	Please fill up (the tank with) petrol.
anleḍeḍ bhar dījiye. अनलेडेड भर दीजिये।	Please fill it up with unleaded.
ḍīzal bhar dījiye. डीज़ल भर दीजिये।	Please fill it up with diesel.

Will you check (look at) the oil? (polite)	***tel dekhẽge?*** तेल देखेंगे?
Will you check (look at) the oil? (informal)	***tel dekhoge?*** तेल देखोगे?
Will you check (look at) the tire pressure? (polite)	***pahiyõ kā preśar dekhẽge?*** पहियों का प्रेशर देखेंगे?
Will you check the tire pressure? (informal)	***pahiyõ kā preśar dekhoge?*** पहियों का प्रेशर देखोगे?
Will you change the oil? (polite)	***āp tel badlẽge?*** आप तेल बदलेंगे?
Will you change the oil? (informal)	***tum tel badloge?*** तुम तेल बदलोगे?
Will you wash (clean) my car? (polite)	***āp merī gāṛī sāf kar dẽge?*** आप मेरी गाड़ी साफ़ कर देंगे?
Will you wash my car? (informal)	***tum merī gāṛī sāf kar doge?*** तुम मेरी गाड़ी साफ़ कर दोगे?

Will you wash (clean) the windshield?* (polite) — ***āp śīśā sāf kar dẽge?*** आप शीशा साफ़ कर देंगे?

Will you wash the windshield?* (informal) — ***tum śīśā sāf kar doge?*** तुम शीशा साफ़ कर दोगे?

5.5 Breakdowns and repairs

merī gāṛī kharāb ho gayī hai. मेरी गाड़ी ख़राब हो गयी है। — My car/vehicle has broken down.

kyā āp merī madad karẽge/karẽgī? क्या आप मेरी मदद करेंगे/करेंगी? — Will you help me? (m/f) (polite)

peṭrol khatm ho gayā hai. पेट्रोल ख़त्म हो गया है। — I have run out of gas. (the petrol is finished)

gāṛī band hai, aur cābī andar hai. गाड़ी बंद है और चाबी अंदर है। — I have locked the keys in the car. (the car is closed, and key is inside)

gāṛī sṭārṭ nahī̃ ho rahī hai. गाड़ी स्टार्ट नहीं हो रही है। — My car/vehicle won't start.

Can you take me to the nearest town? — ***āp mujhe agle nagar tak le calẽge?*** आप मुझे अगले नगर तक ले चलेंगे?

I think that the … is broken. (in my opinion the … is broken) — ***mere khyāl mẽ … kharāb hai.*** मेरे ख़्याल में … ख़राब है।

Can you fix (mend) it?* (polite) — ***kyā āp iskī marammat kar sakẽge?*** क्या आप इसकी मरम्मत कर सकेंगे?

Can you fix it?* (informal) — ***kyā tum iskī marammat kar sakoge?*** क्या तुम इसकी मरम्मत कर सकोगे?

* These sentences are conjugated for a masculine subject.

Can you fix the tire?* (polite)	***kyā āp pahiye kī marammat kar sakẽge?*** क्या आप पहिये की मरम्मत कर सकेंगे?
Can you fix the tire?* (informal)	***kyā tum pahiye kī marammat kar sakoge?*** क्या तुम पहिये की मरम्मत कर सकोगे?
Will you change the tire?* (polite)	***kyā āp pahiyā badlẽge?*** क्या आप पहिया बदलेंगे?
Will you change the tire?* (informal)	***kyā tum pahiyā badloge?*** क्या तुम पहिया बदलोगे?
When will it be fixed?	***kab tak ṭhīk hogā?*** कब तक ठीक होगा?
When will it be ready?	***kab tak taiyār hogā?*** कब तक तैयार होगा?
How much will it cost? (how many monies will attach)	***kitne paise lagẽge?*** कितने पैसे लगेंगे?
Will you give me a receipt?* (polite)	***kyā āp mujhe rasīd dẽge?*** क्या आप मुझे रसीद देंगे?

5.6 Renting a vehicle

I would like to rent a … (m/f)	***maĩ kirāye par … lenā cāhtā/cāhtī hũ.*** मैं किराये पर … लेना चाहता/चाहती हूँ।
Do I need a license for this?	***is ke liye kyā mujhe lāisens cāhiye?*** इसके लिये क्या मुझे लाइसेंस चाहिये?
I want/need it for a full (entire) day. (it is wanted to me)	***mujhe pūre din ke liye cāhiye.*** मुझे पूरे दिन के लिये चाहिये।
I want/need it for a half day. (it is wanted to me)	***mujhe ādhe din ke liye cāhiye.*** मुझे आधे दिन के लिये चाहिये।

* These sentences are conjugated for a masculine subject.

I want/need it for the morning only. (it is wanted to me)	***mujhe sirf subah cāhiye.*** मुझे सिर्फ़ सुबह चाहिये।
I want/need it for a week. (it is wanted to me)	***mujhe ek hafte ke liye cāhiye.*** मुझे एक हफ़्ते के लिये चाहिये।
I want/need it with a driver. (it is wanted to me)	***mujhe gāṛī aur ḍrāīvar donõ cāhiye.*** मुझे गाड़ी और ड्राईवर दोनों चाहिये।
I want/need it without a driver. (it is wanted to me)	***mujhe sirf gāṛī cāhiye, ḍrāīvar nahĩ.*** मुझे सिर्फ़ गाड़ी चाहिये ड्राईवर नहीं।
How much do you charge (take)?* (polite)	***kitne paise lete haĩ?*** कितने पैसे लेते हैं?
What is the rate?* (polite) (what calculation do you apply)	***āp kyā hisāb lagāte haĩ?*** आप क्या हिसाब लगाते हैं?
Shall we stop soon? (after a little delay)	***kyā ham thoṛī der bād rukẽ?*** क्या हम थोड़ी देर बाद रुकें?
Are you hungry? (polite)	***kyā āpko bhūkh lagī hai?*** क्या आपको भूख लगी है?
Are you hungry? (informal)	***kyā tumko bhūkh lagī hai?*** क्या तुमको भूख लगी है?
Are you thirsty? (polite)	***kyā āpko pyās lagī hai?*** क्या आपको प्यास लगी है?
Are you thirsty? (informal)	***kyā tumko pyās lagī hai?*** क्या तुमको प्यास लगी है?
Shall we stop for tea?	***kyā ham cāy pīne rukẽ?*** क्या हम चाय पीने रुकें?

* These sentences are conjugated for a masculine subject.

5.7 Hitchhiking

Where are you going?* (polite)	***āp kahā̃ jā rahe haĩ?*** आप कहाँ जा रहे हैं?
Where are you going?* (informal)	***tum kahā̃ jā rahe ho?*** तुम कहाँ जा रहे हो?
Will you take me to...?* (polite)	***kyā āp mujhe ... le calẽge?*** क्या आप मुझे ... ले चलेंगे?
Will you take me to...?* (informal)	***kyā tum mujhe ... le caloge?*** क्या तुम मुझे ... ले चलोगे?
How far are you going?* (polite)	***āp kitnī dūr jā rahe haĩ?*** आप कितनी दूर जा रहे हैं?
How far are you going?* (informal)	***tum kitnī dūr jā rahe ho?*** तुम कितनी दूर जा रहे हो?
Are you going via ... ?* (polite)	***kyā āp ... se ho kar jā rahe haĩ?*** क्या आप ... से होकर जा रहे हैं?
Are you going via ... ?* (informal)	***kyā tum ... se ho kar jā rahe ho?*** क्या तुम ... से होकर जा रहे हो?
I have to go to	***mujhe ... jānā hai.*** मुझे ... जाना है।
We have to go to	***hamẽ ... jānā hai.*** हमें ... जाना है।
Could you please stop here.	***yahā̃ rukiye.*** यहाँ रुकिये।
Please let me off here. (leave me)	***mujhe yahā̃ choṛ dījiye.*** मुझे यहाँ छोड़ दीजिये।
Thank you for taking me.	***mujhe le jāne ke liye śukriyā.*** मुझे ले जाने के लिये शुक्रिया।

* These sentences are conjugated for a masculine subject.

6 Arrival and Departure

6. Arrival and Departure

6.1 General

Is this train going to ...?	***kyā yeh ṭren ... jā rahī hai?*** क्या यह ट्रेन ... जा रही है?
Is this bus going to ...?	***kyā yeh bas ... jā rahī hai?*** क्या यह बस ... जा रही है?
Does this bus go via ...?	***kyā yeh bas ... se ho kar jātī hai?*** क्या यह बस ... से होकर जाती है?
I want to catch the train to .... (m/f)	***maĩ ... kī ṭren pakaṛnā cāhtā/cāhtī hū̃*** मैं ... की ट्रेन पकड़ना चाहता/चाहती हूँ।
What is the number of the train to ...?	***... kī ṭren kā nambar kyā hai?*** ... की ट्रेन का नंबर क्या है?
Does this train stop at ... station?	***kyā yeh ṭren ... ke sṭeśan par ruktī hai?*** क्या यह ट्रेन ... के स्टेशन पर रुकती है?
How much is the ticket to ...? (in how much does the ticket come)	***...kā ṭikaṭ kitne mẽ ātā hai?*** ... का टिकट कितने में आता है?
I want/need a return ticket.	***mujhe vāpasī ṭikaṭ cāhiye.*** मुझे वापसी टिकट चाहिये।
I have to get down at ...	***mujhe ... par utarnā hai.*** मुझे ... पर उतरना है।

6.2 Customs

We are going to ...	***ham ... jā rahe haĩ.*** हम ... जा रहे हैं।
I am traveling in India. (m) (for traveling I have come)	***maĩ bhārat mẽ ghūmne ke liye āyā hū̃.*** मैं भारत में घूमने के लिये आया हूँ।

I am traveling in India. (f) (for traveling I have come)	***maĩ bhārat mẽ ghūmne ke liye āyī hū̃.*** मैं भारत में घूमने के लिये आयी हूँ।
I have come to do some work. (m/f)	***maĩ kuch kām karne āyā/āyī hū̃*** मैं कुछ काम करने आया/आयी हूँ।
I will stay here for a few days. (m/f)	***maĩ yahā̃ kuch din (ke liye) rahū̃gā/ rahū̃gī.*** मैं यहाँ कुछ दिन (के लिये) रहूँगा/रहूँगी।
I will stay here for a week. (m/f)	***maĩ yahā̃ ek hafte (ke liye) rahū̃gā/ rahū̃gī.*** मैं यहाँ एक हफ़्ते (के लिये) रहूँगा/रहूँगी।
I will stay here for the weekend. (m/f)	***maĩ yahā̃ ek vīkeṇḍ (ke liye) rahū̃gā/ rahū̃gī.*** मैं यहाँ एक वीकेंड (के लिये) रहूँगा/रहूँगी।

6.3 Luggage

Porter!	***porṭar!*** पोर्टर!
How much do you want?* (polite) (how much will you take)	***āp kitnā lẽge?*** आप कितना लेंगे?
How much do you want?* (informal) (how much will you take)	***tum kitnā loge?*** तुम कितना लोगे?
Please pick up this luggage.	***yeh sāmān uṭhāīye.*** यह सामान उठाइये।
Please take it to a taxi. (polite)	***ṭaiksī tak le jāiye.*** टैक्सी तक ले जाइये।
Please take it to a taxi. (informal)	***ṭaiksī tak le jāo.*** टैक्सी तक ले जाओ।
Please take it to an autorickshaw. (polite)	***āṭo tak le jāiye.*** ऑटो तक ले जाइये।

* These sentences are conjugated for a masculine subject.

Please take it to an autorickshaw. (informal)	***āṭo tak le jāo.*** ऑटो तक ले जाओ।
How much per piece?* (polite)	***ek pīs ke liye kitnā lete haĩ?*** एक पीस के लिये कितना लेते हैं?
How much per piece?* (informal)	***ek pīs ke liye kitnā lete ho?*** एक पीस के लिये कितना लेते हो?
May I keep my luggage somewhere? (m/f)	***kyā maĩ apnā sāmān kahī̃ rakh saktā/saktī hū̃?*** क्या मैं अपना सामान कहीं रख सकता/सकती हूँ?
This is not my luggage.	***yeh merā sāmān nahī̃ hai.*** यह मेरा सामान नहीं है।
Is there a place to store luggage here?	***kyā yahā̃ sāmān rakhne kī jagah hai?*** क्या यहाँ सामान रखने की जगह है?

6.4 Questions to passengers

Ticket types

First or second class?	***pratham yā dvitīya śreṇī?*** प्रथम या द्वितीय श्रेणी?
One-way or return (two-way)?	***ek-tarafā yā do-tarafā?*** एक-तरफ़ा या दो-तरफ़ा?
Near the window?	***khiṛkī ke pās?*** खिड़की के पास?
Sleeper class? (sleeping's berth)	***sone kā barth?*** सोने का बर्थ?
Top, middle or bottom?	***ūpar kā, bīc kā, yā nīce kā barth?*** ऊपर का, बीच का, या नीचे का बर्थ?
How many tickets?	***kitne ṭikaṭ?*** कितने टिकट?
How many travelers?	***kitne yātrī?*** कितने यात्री?

* These sentences are conjugated for a masculine subject.

Destination

Where do you want to go? (m/f) (polite)	***āp kahā̃ jānā cāhte/cāhtī haĩ?*** आप कहाँ जाना चाहते/चाहती हैं?
When do you want to go? (m/f) (polite)	***āp kab jānā cāhte/cāhtī haĩ?*** आप कब जाना चाहते/चाहती हैं?
Your (train) leaves (at 8 o'clock). (polite)	***āp kī (gāṛī) (āṭh baje) chūṭtī hai.*** आप की (गाड़ी) (आठ बजे) छूटती है।
You will have to get off (down) at .... (polite)	***āpko ... par utarnā hogā.*** आपको ... पर उतरना होगा।
You will have to go via.... (polite)	***āpko ... se ho kar jānā hogā.*** आपको ... से होकर जाना होगा।
You will then go to ... (on the 8th) (m/f) (polite)	***phir āp (āṭh tārī<u>kh</u> ko) ... jāẽge/jāẽgī.*** फिर आप (आठ तारीख़ को) ... जाएँगे/जाएँगी।
You will depart (on the 8th). (m/f) (polite)	***āp (āṭh tārī<u>kh</u> ko) ravānā hõge/hõgī.*** आप (आठ तारीख़ को) रवाना होंगे/होंगी।
You will return (on the 8th). (m/f) (polite)	***āp (āṭh tārī<u>kh</u> ko) vāpas āẽge/āẽgī.*** आप (आठ तारीख़ को) वापस आएँगे/आएँगी।

Inside the vehicle

ṭikaṭ dikhāiye. टिकट दिखाइये।	Please show me your ticket.
pāsporṭ dikhāiye. पासपोर्ट दिखाइये।	Please show me you passport.
yeh āpkī kursī nahī̃ hai. यह आपकी कुरसी नहीं है।	This is not your seat. (polite)
āpkā ṭikaṭ ṭhīk nahī̃ hai. आपका टिकट ठीक नहीं है।	You have the wrong ticket. (polite)

yeh ṭikaṭ āj kī tārīkh kā nahī̃ hai. यह टिकट आज की तारीख़ का नहीं है।	You are traveling on the wrong date.
āpko jurmānā denā hogā. आपको जुर्माना देना होगा।	You will have to pay a fine. (polite)
ṭren ... ghanṭe der se jāegī. ट्रेन ... घंटे देर से जाएगी।	The train is delayed by ....

6.5 Tickets

Where is the booking office?	***buking āfis kahā̃ hai?*** बुकिंग ऑफ़िस कहाँ है?
Where can I book a ticket?	***ṭikaṭ kī buking kahā̃ karāū̃?*** टिकट की बुकिंग कहाँ कराऊँ?
Where can I book a flight?	***flāiṭ kī buking kahā̃ karāū̃?*** फ़्लाइट की बुकिंग कहाँ कराऊँ?
Where can I reserve a seat?	***sīṭ kā ārakṣaṇ kahā̃ karāū̃?*** सीट का आरक्षण कहाँ कराऊँ?
I need a one-way ticket. (to me is needed)	***mujhe ek-tarafā ṭikaṭ cāhiye.*** मुझे एक-तरफ़ा टिकट चाहिये।
Please give me a return ticket.	***do-tarafā ṭikaṭ dījiye.*** दो-तरफ़ा टिकट दीजिये।
Please give me a first class ticket.	***pratham śreṇī kā ṭikaṭ dījiye.*** प्रथम श्रेणी का टिकट दीजिये।
Please give me a second class ticket.	***dvitīya śreṇī kā ṭikaṭ dījiye.*** द्वितीय श्रेणी का टिकट दीजिये।
I want to make a reservation. (m/f)	***maĩ ārakṣaṇ karānā cāhtā/cāhtī hū̃.*** मैं आरक्षण कराना चाहता/चाहती हूँ।
I want a top, middle, bottom berth.	***mujhe ūpar kā, bīc kā, nīce kā barth cāhiye.*** मुझे ऊपर का, बीच का, नीचे का बर्थ चाहिये।

Please give me a seat near the window.	***mujhe khiṛkī ke pās kī sīṭ dījiye.*** मुझे खिड़की के पास की सीट दीजिये।
Please give me a seat on the side.	***mujhe kinārevālī sīṭ dījiye.*** मुझे किनारेवाली सीट दीजिये।
Please give us … tickets.	***hamẽ … ṭikaṭ dījiye.*** हमें … टिकट दीजिये।
Is there a foreign tourist quota on this train?	***kyā is ṭren mẽ ṭūrisṭ koṭā hai?*** क्या इस ट्रेन में टूरिस्ट कोटा है?

6.6 Information

Please give me a time table.	***mujhe ṭāim ṭebal/samay sārṇī dījiye.*** मुझे टाइम टेबल/समय सारणी दीजिये।
Where is a time table available? (where will a time table be found)	***ṭāim ṭebal/samay sārṇī kahā̃ milegā/ milegī.*** टाइम टेबल/ समय सारणी कहाँ मिलेगा/मिलेगी?
Where is the bus terminus?	***bas kā aḍḍā kahā̃ hai?*** बस का अड्डा कहाँ है?
Where is the train station?	***sṭeśan kahā̃ hai?*** स्टेशन कहाँ है?

maĩ ṭikaṭ kanfarm karnā cāhtā/cāhtī hū̃. मैं टिकट कन्फ़र्म करना चाहता/चाहती हूँ।	I want to confirm my ticket. (m/f)
maĩ ṭikaṭ kainsal karānā cāhtā/cāhtī hū̃. मैं टिकट कैंसल कराना चाहता/चाहती हूँ।	I want to cancel my ticket. (m/f)
maĩ … jānā cāhtā/cāhtī hū̃. मैं … जाना चाहता/चाहती हूँ।	I want to go to … (m/f)
maĩ vahā̃ sīdhe jānā cāhtā/cāhtī hū̃. मैं वहाँ सीधे जाना चाहता/चाहती हूँ।	I want to go straight there. (m/f)
ek-tarafā ṭikaṭ kitne mẽ ātā hai? एक-तरफ़ा टिकट कितने में आता है?	How much is a one-way ticket?

do-tarafā ṭikaṭ kitne mẽ ātā hai? दो-तरफ़ा टिकट कितने में आता है?	How much is a return ticket?
kyā maĩ rāste mẽ ruk saktā/saktī hũ? क्या मैं रास्ते में रुक सकता/सकती हूँ?	Can I stop on route? (in the middle) (m/f)
kyā mujhe zyādā paise dene hõge? क्या मुझे ज़्यादा पैसे देने होंगे?	Will I have to pay extra (more) money?

Is this an express train?	***kyā yeh ekspres gāṛī hai?*** क्या यह एक्स्प्रेस गाड़ी है?
Will I have to change trains?	***kyā mujhe gāṛī badalnī hogī?*** क्या मुझे गाड़ी बदलनी होगी?
Does the boat stop anywhere else?	***kyā nāv kahĩ aur ruktī hai?*** क्या नाव कहीं और रुकती है?
Does this bus/train stop at…?	***kyā yeh bas/ṭren … par ruktī hai?*** क्या यह बस/ट्रेन … पर रुकती है?
Where do I have to get off?	***mujhe kahā̃ utarnā hogā?*** मुझे कहाँ उतरना होगा?
How will I go from there?	***vahā̃ se maĩ kaise jaū̃gā/jāū̃gī?*** वहाँ से मैं कैसे जाऊँगा/जाऊँगी?
How long will I have to wait (stop)?	***mujhe kitnī der ruknā hogā?*** मुझे कितनी देर रुकना होगा?
When will the … leave? (m/f)	***… kab chūṭegā/chūṭegī?*** … कब छूटेगा/छूटेगी?
When is the first bus/train?	***pehlī bas/ṭren kab hai?*** पहली बस/ट्रेन कब है?
When is the last (final) bus/train?	***ā<u>kh</u>irī bas/ṭren kab hai?*** आख़िरी बस/ट्रेन कब है?
How long does it take to get there?	***jāne mẽ kitnī der lagtī hai?*** जाने में कितनी देर लगती है?
What time does the flight/train/bas arrive?	***uṛān/ṭren/bas kitne baje pahũctī hai?*** उड़ान/ट्रेन/बस कितने बजे पहुँचती है?

From where does the train to … depart?	*… jānevālī ṭren kahā̃ se chūṭtī hai?* … जानेवाली ट्रेन कहाँ से छूटती है?

6.7 Airports

● **The major** airports in India are steadily being upgraded. The international airports in New Delhi and Mumbai, in particular, are world-class, having been renovated at the beginning of the twenty-first century. There are several modes of transport from the Delhi airport, but if you plan to catch a taxi, a safe, convenient and comfortable method is to go to the pre-paid taxi booth (operated by the Delhi Traffic Police) just outside the international terminal.

International
antarrāṣṭrīya
अंतर्राष्ट्रीय

Domestic
antardeśīya
अंतर्देशीय

Departures (m)
prasthān
प्रस्थान

Arrivals (m)
āgaman
आगमन

Immigration (m)
apravāsan
अप्रवासन

Toilets (m)
śaucālay
शौचालय

Transfer (international/domestic) (m)
(antarrāṣṭrīya/antardeśīya) sthānāntaraṇ
(अंतर्राष्ट्रीय/अंतर्देशीय) स्थानांतरण

No Smoking (smoking forbidden)
dhūmrapān niṣedh
धूम्रपान निषेध

6.8 Trains

● **Indian Railways** is owned and operated by the Indian Government. It is the largest employer in the country, and even has its own annual budget, which is separate from the budget for the other services controlled by the Central Government. It carries over twenty-five million passengers on the suburban and intercity networks on a daily basis. It is one of the most enjoyable ways to see the country, if you have the time to travel by this means. There are many types of trains, some faster than others, and some for which a reservation is needed well in advance.

The most comfortable and modern trains are the Shatabdis and Rajdhanis. Shatabdi ('century') trains run between major cities and are not overnight trains, whereas Rajdhani ('capital') trains run overnight between Delhi and major provincial cities. For both of these trains, a reserved ticket is essential. Many main railway stations in major cities have a Foreign Tourist Booking Office where tourists traveling in India can book tickets on selected trains in a special tourist quota. There are two classes of booking, first class and second class.

6.9 Taxis

mujhe ... jānā hai. मुझे ... जाना है।	I have to go to ...
mujhe ṭaiksī cāhiye. मुझे टैक्सी चाहिये।	I need a taxi.
kyā āp ṭaiksī bulāẽge/bulāẽgī? क्या आप टैक्सी बुलाएँगे/बुलाएँगी?	Will you call (summon) me a taxi? (m/f)
mīṭar lagāẽge? मीटर लगाएँगे?	Will you go by the meter? (polite)
mīṭar lagāoge? मीटर लगाओगे?	Will you go by the meter? (m/f) (informal) (will you apply the meter)
mīṭar cālū kījiye. मीटर चालू कीजिये।	Please start the meter. (polite)
havāī aḍḍe jānā hai. हवाई अड्डे जाना है।	I have to go to the airport.

I am late.	***mujhe der ho gayī hai.*** मुझे देर हो गयी है।
I have to get there quickly.	***mujhe jaldī pahũcnā hai.*** मुझे जल्दी पहुँचना है।

Please hurry. (polite) (please drive fast)	***āp tez calāiye.*** आप तेज़ चलाइये।
Hurry. (informal)	***tez calāo.*** तेज़ चलाओ।
Please go straight. (polite)	***āp sīdhe caliye.*** आप सीधे चलिये।
Go straight. (informal)	***sīdhe calo.*** सीधे चलो।
Please turn right. (polite)	***dāhinī taraf moṛiye.*** दाहिनी तरफ़ मोड़िये।
Turn right. (informal)	***dāhinī taraf moṛo.*** दाहिनी तरफ़ मोड़ो।
Please turn left. (polite)	***bāyī̃ taraf moṛiye.*** बायीं तरफ़ मोड़िये।
Turn right. (informal)	***bāyī̃ taraf moṛo.*** बायीं तरफ़ मोड़ो।
Please stop here. (polite)	***yahā̃ rukiye.*** यहाँ रुकिये।
Stop here. (informal)	***yahā̃ ruko.*** यहाँ रुको।
Please wait for five minutes. (polite)	***pā̃c minaṭ rukiye.*** पाँच मिनट रुकिये।
Wait for five minutes. (informal)	***pā̃c minaṭ ruko.*** पाँच मिनट रुको।

7 A Place to Stay

7. A Place to Stay

7.1 General

āp kitne din rahẽge/rahẽgī? आप कितने दिन रहेंगे/रहेंगी?	How long will you stay? (m/f) (polite) (how many days)
fārm bhar dījiye. फ़ॉर्म भर दीजिये।	Please fill in this form.
pāsporṭ dikhāiye. पासपोर्ट दिखाइये।	Please show your passport.
abhī bhugtān karnā hogā. अभी भुगतान करना होगा।	You will have to pay in advance. (you will have to pay right now)
ḍipāziṭ denā hogā. डिपॉज़िट देना होगा।	You will have to pay a deposit.

My name is …	***merā nām … hai.*** मेरा नाम … है।
I have a booking.	***merī būking hai.*** मेरी बुकिंग है।
How much is the room?	***kamrā kitne kā hai?*** कमरा कितने का है?
What is the rate (rental) for one day?	***ek din kā kirāyā kitnā hai?*** एक दिन का किराया कितना है?
How many days can we stay?	***ham kitne din ṭhehar sakẽge?*** हम कितने दिन ठहर सकेंगे?
I don't know how many days I will stay. (m/f)	***mujhe mālūm nahī̃ ki kitne din ṭhehrū̃gā/ṭhehrū̃gī.*** मुझे मालूम नहीं कि कितने दिन ठहरूँगा/ठहरूँगी।
Is there twenty-four hour hot water?	***kyā caubīs ghanṭe garm pānī miltā hai?*** क्या चौबीस घंटे गर्म पानी मिलता है?

7.2 Hotels/guest houses

Is there a single room available?	***singal kamrā milegā?*** सिंगल कमरा मिलेगा?
Is there a double room available?	***ḍabal kamrā milegā?*** डबल कमरा मिलेगा?
How much is it per person?	***ek ādmī ke rehne ke kitne paise lete haĩ?*** एक आदमी के रहने के कितने पैसे लेते हैं?
Is food included?	***kyā is mẽ khānā bhī śāmil hai?*** क्या इस में खाना भी शामिल है?
Is breakfast included?	***kyā nāśtā śāmil hai?*** क्या नाश्ता शामिल है?
Is lunch included?	***kyā din kā khānā śāmil hai?*** क्या दिन का खाना शामिल है?
Is dinner included?	***kyā rāt kā khānā śāmil hai?*** क्या रात का खाना शामिल है?
We want ajoining rooms.	***hamẽ agal-bagal vāle kamre cāhiye.*** हमें अगल-बगल वाले कमरे चाहिये।
Please give us a room with a bathroom.	***bāthrūmvālā kamrā dījiye.*** बाथरूम वाला कमरा दीजिये।
Is there … in the hotel?	***hoṭal mẽ … hai?*** होटल में … है?
Do you have room service?	***kyā rūm sarvis hai?*** क्या रूम सरविस है?
Please show me the room.	***kamrā dikhāiye.*** कमरा दिखाइये।
Please take me to the room.	***kamre mẽ le jāiye.*** कमरे में ले जाइये।
I will take this room. (m/f)	***maĩ yeh kamrā lũgā/lũgī.*** मैं यह कमरा लूँगा/लूँगी।
Please show me another room.	***koī dūsrā kamrā dikhāiye.*** कोई दूसरा कमरा दिखाइये।

We don't like this room.	***hamẽ yeh kamrā pasand nahī̃ hai.*** हमें यह कमरा पसंद नहीं है।
I don't like this room.	***mujhe yeh kamrā pasand nahī̃ hai.*** मुझे यह कमरा पसंद नहीं है।
Do you have a cheaper room?	***kyā is se sastā kamrā hai?*** क्या इससे सस्ता कमरा है?
Do you have a more expensive room?	***kyā is se mahẽgā kamrā hai?*** क्या इससे महँगा कमरा है?
Will you put in an extra bed?	***kyā āp ek aur cārpāī lagāẽge?*** क्या आप एक और चारपाई लगाएँगे?
What time is breakfast?	***nāśtā kitne baje hotā hai?*** नाश्ता कितने बजे होता है?
Where is the dining hall?	***ḍāining hāl kahā̃ hai?*** डाइनिंग हॉल कहाँ है?
Can I eat breakfast in the room?	***kyā maĩ nāśtā kamre mẽ kar saktā/ saktī hū̃?*** क्या मैं नाश्ता कमरे में कर सकता/सकती हूँ?
Please give me my key.	***cābī dījiye.*** चाबी दीजिये।
Please give me the key to room …	***… nambar kamre kī cābī dījiye.*** … नम्बर कमरे की चाबी दीजिये।
Please put this in the safe.	***ise tijorī mẽ rakhiye.*** इसे तिजोरी में रखिये।
Please wake me at (5) A.M. (rouse me)	***(pā̃c) baje subah mujhe uṭhāiye.*** (पाँच) बजे सुबह मुझे उठाइये।
Please give me another blanket.	***ek aur kambal dījiye.*** एक और कम्बल दीजिये।
Please give me clean sheets.	***sāf cādarẽ dījiye.*** साफ़ चादरें दीजिये।
What time is the room cleaned?	***kamrā kitne baje sāf karte haĩ?*** कमरा कितने बजे साफ़ करते हैं?

7.3 Complaints

There is a lot of noise outside the room.	***kamre ke bāhar bahut śorgul hai.*** कमरे के बाहर बहुत शोरगुल है।
Please turn down the T.V. (reduce the T.V.'s sound)	***ṭī. vī. kī āvāz kam kījiye.*** टी० वी० की आवाज़ कम कीजिये।
Please make less noise	***śorghul kam kījiye.*** शोरगुल कम कीजिये।
Please give (us) toilet paper.	***ṭāyleṭ pepar dījiye.*** टॉयलेट पेपर दीजिये।
The toilet doesn't work properly.	***ṭāyleṭ ṭhīk se kām nahī̃ kartā.*** टॉयलेट ठीक से काम नहीं करता।
The water heater (geyser) is broken.	***gīzar kharāb hai.*** गीज़र ख़राब है।
There is no hot water in the room.	***kamre mẽ garm pānī nahī̃ hai.*** कमरे में गर्म पानी नहीं है।
There is no soap in the room.	***kamre mẽ sābun nahī̃ hai.*** कमरे में साबुन नहीं है।
Please give us soap.	***hamẽ sābun dījiye.*** हमें साबुन दीजिये।
The room is not clean.	***kamrā sāf nahī̃ hai.*** कमरा साफ़ नहीं है।
The room is very cold.	***kamre mẽ bahut ṭhaṇḍ hai.*** कमरे में बहुत ठंड है।
The windows don't open.	***khiṛkiyā̃ nahī̃ khultī̃.*** खिड़कियाँ नहीं खुलतीं।
The bed is broken.	***palang kharāb hai.*** पलंग ख़राब है।
There are many mosquitos in the room.	***kamre mẽ bahut macchar haĩ.*** कमरे में बहुत मच्छर हैं।
Please give me a mosquito net.	***macchardānī dījiye.*** मच्छरदानी दीजिये।

7.4 Departure

I am leaving (going) tomorrow. (m)	***maĩ kal jā rahā hū̃.*** मैं कल जा रहा हूँ।
I am leaving (going) tomorrow. (f)	***maĩ kal jā rahī hū̃.*** मैं कल जा रही हूँ।
We are going tomorrow.	***ham kal jā rahe haĩ.*** हम कल जा रहे हैं।
I want to pay the bill. (m/f)	***maĩ bil cukānā cāhtā/cāhtī hū̃.*** मैं बिल चुकाना चाहता/चाहती हूँ।
Can we check out late?	***kyā ham der se cek āuṭ kar sakẽge?*** क्या हम देर से चेक आउट कर सकेंगे?
Can we vacant the room late?	***kyā ham der se kamrā khālī kar sakẽge?*** क्या हम देर से कमरा ख़ाली कर सकेंगे?
Please return my passport/deposit.	***pāsporṭ/ḍipāziṭ vāpas kījiye.*** पासपोर्ट/डिपॉज़िट वापस कीजिये।
We are in a hurry.	***hamẽ bahut jaldī hai.*** हमें बहुत जल्दी है।
Can we leave some luggage here (for two weeks)?	***kyā ham (do hafte ke liye) kuch sāmān yahā̃ choṛ sakẽge?*** क्या हम (दो हफ़्ते के लिये) कुछ सामान यहाँ छोड़ सकेंगे?
We will definitely return.	***ham zarūr vāpas āẽge.*** हम ज़रूर वापस आएँगे।
I will definitely return. (m/f)	***maĩ zarūr vāpas āū̃gā/āū̃gī.*** मैं ज़रूर वापस आऊँगा/आऊँगी।
I really enjoyed it here.	***yahā̃ mujhe bahut acchā lagā.*** यहाँ मुझे बहुत अच्छा लगा।

8 Money Matters

8. Money Matters

● **In general** banks in India are open from 9 A.M. until 6 P.M., although customer service hours can be shorter than this. Often banks are also open on Saturdays, for reduced hours. Almost all of India's major banks now have numerous ATMS, and there is generally no difficulty withdrawing money from overseas accounts from these ATMs.

8.1 Banks

Where is the bank?	***baink kahā̃ hai?*** बैंक कहाँ है?
Is there an ATM close by?	***kyā koī e. ṭī. em. nazdīk hai?*** क्या कोई ए० टी० एम० नज़दीक है?
Can I withdraw money on my credit card? (take money by credit card) (m/f)	***kyā yahā̃ kreḍiṭ kārḍ se paise nikāl saktā/saktī hū̃?*** क्या यहाँ क्रेडिट कार्ड से पैसे निकाल सकता/सकती हूँ?
How much money can I withdraw? (m/f)	***kitne paise nikāl saktā/saktī hū̃?*** कितने पैसे निकाल सकता/सकती हूँ।
The machine swallowed my card. (became stuck)	***maśīn mẽ merā kārḍ phā̃s gayā.*** मशीन में मेरा कार्ड फँस गया।
I would like to change some money. (m/f)	***maĩ paise badalnā cāhtā/cahtī hū̃.*** मैं पैसे बदलना चाहता/चाहती हूँ।
I have American dollars.	***mere pās amrīkī ḍālar haĩ.*** मेरे पास अमरीकी डॉलर हैं।

yahā̃ hastākṣar kījiye. यहाँ हस्ताक्षर कीजिये।	Sign here, please.
yeh fārm bhar dījiye. यह फ़ॉर्म भर दीजिये।	Fill out this form, please.

pāsporṭ dikhāiye. पासपोर्ट दिखाइये।	Please show me your passport.
kreḍiṭ kārḍ dikhāiye. क्रेडिट कार्ड दिखाइये।	Please show me your credit card.
ḍebiṭ kārḍ dikhāiye. डेबिट कार्ड दिखाइये।	Please show me your debit card.
āī. ḍī. kārḍ dikhāiye. आई० डी० कार्ड दिखाइये।	Please show me your I.D. card.

8.2 Settling the bill

Could you put this on my bill.	***mere bil mẽ joṛ dījiye.*** मेरे बिल में जोड़ दीजिये।
Should I give a tip?	***kyā mujhe bakhśīś denī cāhiye?*** क्या मुझे बख़्शीश देनी चाहिये?
Can I pay by credit card? (m/f)	***kyā maĩ kreḍiṭ kārḍ se bhugtān kar saktā/saktī hū̃?*** क्या मैं क्रेडिट कार्ड से भुगतान कर सकता/सकती हूँ?
Can I pay in U.S. dollars? (m/f)	***kyā maĩ amrīkī ḍālar se bhugtān kar saktā/saktī hū̃?*** क्या मैं अमरीकी डॉलर से भुगतान कर सकता/सकती हूँ।
You have given me too much money.	***āpne mujhe zyādā paise diye haĩ.*** आपने मुझे ज़्यादा पैसे दिये हैं।
You haven't given me back enough money.	***āpne mujhe kam paise diye haĩ.*** आपने मुझे कम पैसे दिये हैं।
Please re-check my account. (re attach my account)	***hisāb phir se lagāiye.*** हिसाब फिर से लगाइये।
Please give me a receipt.	***rasīd dījiye.*** रसीद दीजिये।

I don't have enough money.	***mere pās kāfī paise nahī̃ haĩ.*** मेरे पास काफ़ी पैसे नहीं हैं।
Please take the money.	***paise lījiye.*** पैसे लीजिये।
Please give me back the money.	***paise vāpas kījiye.*** पैसे वापस कीजिये।

8.3 Business terms

I work online. (m/f)	***maĩ ān-lāin kām kartā/kartī hū̃.*** मैं ऑन-लाइन काम करता/करती हूँ।
I have experience. (to me experience is)	***mujhe anubhav hai.*** मुझे अनुभव है।
Is the manager here?	***kyā prabandhak yahā̃ par haĩ?*** क्या प्रबंधक यहाँ पर हैं?
I would like to meet the owner of the company. (m/f)	***maĩ kampanī ke mālik se milnā cāhtā/cāhtī hū̃.*** मैं कम्पनी के मालिक से मिलना चाहता/चाहती हूँ।

company (f)
kampanī
कम्पनी

businessman/person (m)
vyāpārī
व्यापारी

importation (m)
āyāt
आयात

exportation (m)
niryāt
निर्यात

owner of the company (m)
kampanī ke mālik
कम्पनी के मालिक

manager (m)
prabandhak
प्रबंधक

multinational corporation (f)
bahurāṣṭrīya kampanī
बहुराष्ट्रीय कम्पनी

C.V. (f)
sī. vī.
सी० वी०

profession (m)
peśā
पेशा

professional
peśevar
पेशेवर

specialist/expert (m)
viśeṣagya
विशेषज्ञ

certificate (m)
pramān patra
प्रमाण पत्र

contract (m)
anubandh
अनुबंध

qualified
dakṣ
दक्ष

rate (f)
dar
दर

exchange rate (f)
vinimay dar
विनिमय दर

gratuity, tip (f)
bakhśiś
बख़्शिश

application (f)
arzī
अर्ज़ी

account (m)
khātā
खाता

job (f)
naukrī
नौकरी

degree (f)
upādhi
उपाधि

investment (m)
niveś
निवेश

payment (m)
bhugtān
भुगतान

interview (m)
iṇṭarvyū
इंटरव्यू

promotion (f)
padonnati
पदोन्नति

official (m)
adhikārī
अधिकारी

training (m)
praśikṣaṇ
प्रशिक्षण

salary (m)
vetan
वेतन

exchange (m)
vinimay
विनिमय

advance (f)
peśagī
पेशगी

office (m)
kāryālay
कार्यालय

employee (m)
karmcārī
कर्मचारी

statement (m)
bayān
बयान

9 Mail, Phone and Internet

9. Mail, Phone and Internet

9.1 Mail

stamps (m/f) ***ṭikaṭ*** टिकट	telegram (m) ***tār*** तार
parcel (m) ***pārsal*** पार्सल	money order (m) ***manī ārḍar*** मनी ऑर्डर

Where is...? — ***... kahā̃ hai?***
... कहाँ है?

–the nearest post office — ***sab se nazdīk ḍāk khānā***
सब से नज़दीक डाकख़ाना

–the main post office — ***jī. pī. o.***
जी० पी० ओ०

mujhe kis khiṛkī par jānā cāhiye?
मुझे किस खिड़की पर जाना चाहिये?
To which counter (window) should I go?

ciṭṭhī kahā̃ ḍālū̃?
चिट्ठी कहाँ डालूँ?
Where may I post a letter?

ṭikaṭ kahā̃ kharīd sakū̃gā/sakū̃gī?
टिकट कहाँ ख़रीद सकूँगा/सकूँगी?
Where can I buy stamps? (m/f)

pārsal lene kahā̃ jānā cāhiye?
पार्सल लेने कहाँ जाना चाहिये?
Where should I pick up a parcel?

yahā̃ pārsal kahā̃ banvā sakte haĩ?
यहाँ पॉर्सल कहाँ बनवा सकते हैं?
Where can I have a parcel wrapped?

... bhejne mẽ kitne paise lagẽge?
... भेजने में कितने पैसे लगेंगे?
How much to send this to ...?

kyā is mẽ kāfī ṭikaṭ lage haĩ?
क्या इसमें काफ़ी टिकट लगे हैं?
Are there enough stamps on this?

I would like to buy some stamps. (m/f)	***maĩ kuch ṭikaṭ <u>kh</u>arīdnā cāhtā/cāhtī hū̃.*** मैं कुछ टिकट ख़रीदना चाहता/चाहती हूँ।
I want to send this ... (m/f)	***maĩ yeh ... bhejnā cāhtā/cāhtī hū̃.*** मैं यह ... भेजना चाहता/चाहती हूँ।
by express post	***ekspres posṭ se*** एक्स्प्रेस पोस्ट से
by air mail	***havāī ḍāk se*** हवाई डाक से
by registered post	***rajisṭarḍ posṭ se*** रजिस्टर्ड पोस्ट से

9.2 Telephone

Is there a public call office around here?	***kyā yahā̃ ke āspās pī. sī. o. hai?*** क्या यहाँ के आसपास पी० सी० ओ० है?
May I make a call?	***kyā maĩ ek fon karū̃?*** क्या मैं एक फ़ोन करूँ?
Where can I get a mobile phone?	***mobāil fon kahā̃ milegā?*** मोबाइल फ़ोन कहाँ मिलेगा?
What's the area code for...?	***... kā koḍ kyā hai?*** ... का कोड क्या है?

What's the international access code?	***antarrāṣṭrīya fon karne ke liye kyā nambar lagāte haĩ?*** अंतर्राष्ट्रीय फ़ोन करने के लिये क्या नम्बर लगाते हैं?
Is this number correct?	***kyā yeh nambar ṭhīk hai?*** क्या यह नम्बर ठीक है?
Should I dial '0' (zero) first?	***kyā pehle 'śūnya' milānā cāhiye?*** क्या पहले 'शून्य' मिलाना चाहिये?
Have there been any phone calls for me? (did any call come for me)	***mere liye koī fon āyā?*** मेरे लिये कोई फ़ोन आया?
What is the charge per minute? (every minute how many paise attach)	***har minaṭ ke kitne paise lagte haĩ?*** हर मिनट के कितने पैसे लगते हैं?

mobile phone (m) ***mobāil fon*** मोबाइल फ़ोन	battery (m) ***sel*** सेल	phone card (m) ***fon kārḍ*** फ़ोन कार्ड
charger (m) ***cārjar*** चार्जर	sim card (m) ***sim kārḍ*** सिम कार्ड	public phone (m) ***pī. sī. o.*** पी० सी० ओ०

The conversation

namaste, maĩ … bol rahā hū̃. नमस्ते, मैं ... बोल रहा हूँ।	Hello, this is… (speaking) (m)
namaste, maĩ … bol rahī hū̃. नमस्ते, मैं ... बोल रही हूँ।	Hello, this is… (speaking) (f)
āp kaun bol rahe haĩ? आप कौन बोल रहे हैं?	Who is speaking? (m) (who are you speaking)
āp kaun bol rahī haĩ? आप कौन बोल रही हैं?	Who is speaking? (f)
kyā maĩ … se bāt karū̃? क्या मैं ... से बात करूँ?	May I talk to (with) ….

māf kījiye, mainne <u>gh</u>alat nambar milāyā. माफ़ कीजिये, मैंने ग़लत नम्बर मिलाया।	Sorry, I have dialed the wrong number.

Do you speak English? (does English come to you)	***kyā āpko angrezī ātī hai?*** क्या आपको अंग्रेज़ी आती है?
Please speak in English.	***angrezī mẽ boliye.*** अंग्रेज़ी में बोलिये।
Please take down my number. (please note my number)	***merā nambar noṭ kījiye.*** मेरा नम्बर नोट कीजिये।
My number is …	***merā nambar …hai.*** मेरा नम्बर ... है।
Please tell him/her I called.	***unhẽ batāiye ki maĩne fon kiyā.*** उन्हें बताइये कि मैंने फ़ोन किया।
I will call again tomorrow. (m/f)	***kal maĩ dubārā fon karũgā/karũgī.*** कल मैं दुबारा फ़ोन करूँगा/करूँगी।
There is a phone call for you. (your phone is)	***āpkā fon hai.*** आपका फ़ोन है।
You have to dial '0' first.	***pehle 'śūnya' milāiye.*** पहले 'शून्य' मिलाइये।
One moment, please.	***ek minaṭ holḍ kījiye.*** एक मिनट होल्ड कीजिये।
There's no answer.	***koī nahĩ uṭhā rahā hai.*** कोई नहीं उठा रहा है।
The line is busy.	***lāin bizī hai.*** लाइन बिज़ी है।
Do you want to wait? (m/f)	***āp ruknā cāhte/cāhtī hai?*** आप रुकना चाहते/चाहती हैं?

You have dialed the wrong number.	***āpne ghalat nambar milāyā.*** आपने ग़लत नम्बर मिलाया।
He/she is not here right now. (polite)	***abhī vo yahā̃ nahī̃ haĩ.*** अभी वे यहाँ नहीं हैं।

9.3 Internet/email

What is your email address? (polite)	***āpkā ī-mel kā patā kyā hai?*** आपका ई-मेल का पता क्या है?
Do you use …? (m/f) (polite)	***kyā āp … kā istemāl karte/kartī haĩ?*** क्या आप … का इस्तेमाल करते/करती हैं?
May I use your computer? (m/f)	***kyā maĩ āpke kampyūṭar kā istemāl kar saktā/saktī hū̃?*** क्या मैं आपके कम्प्यूटर का इस्तेमाल कर सकता/सकती हूँ?
I sent you an email.	***maĩne āpko ī-mel bhejī.*** मैंने आपको ई-मेल भेजी।
I am online.	***maĩ ān-lāin hū̃.*** मैं ऑन-लाइन हूँ।
The connection was lost.	***kanekśan kaṭ gayā.*** कनेक्शन कट गया।
The speed of the Internet is slow.	***inṭarneṭ kī gati dhīmī hai.*** इंटरनेट की गति धीमी है।

Internet (m) ***inṭarneṭ/indrajāl*** इंटरनेट/इंद्रजाल	computer (m) ***kampyūṭar*** कम्प्यूटर	laptop (m) ***laipṭāp*** लैपटॉप
email (f) ***ī-mel*** ई-मेल	virus (m) ***vāiras*** वाइरस	web browser (m) ***veb brāuzar*** वेब ब्राउज़र
download (m) ***ḍāūnloḍ*** डाउनलोड	Facebook (m) ***fesbuk*** फ़ेसबुक	Twitter (m) ***ṭviṭar*** ट्विटर

install
inṣṭāl karnā
इनस्टाल करना

scanner (m)
skainar
स्कैनर

search
talāś karnā
तलाश करना

printer (m)
priṇṭar
प्रिंटर

Internet café
inṭarneṭ kaife
इंटरनेट कैफ़े

spam
spaim
स्पैम

chat
caiṭiṅg karnā
चैटिंग करना

10 Shopping

10. Shopping

● **Shops in** most large cities open at 10 A.M. in the morning and stay open until after 6 P.M. in the evening. In most markets shops remain closed on Sundays. Until recently, particular markets would remain closed on different days, and not necessarily on Sundays. These days, however, if shops are closed on any day of the week, it is likely to be Sundays.

grocery store (f)
parcūn kī dukān
परचून की दुकान

barber (m)
nāī
नाई

bookstore (f)
kitāb kī dukān
किताब की दुकान

butcher's shop (f)
kasāī kī dukān
कसाई की दुकान

cobbler (m)
mocī
मोची

market (m)
bāzār
बाज़ार

pharmacy (m)
davākhānā
दवाख़ाना

cloth shop (f)
kapṛe kī dukān
कपड़े की दुकान

tailor (m)
darzī
दर्ज़ी

household goods (m)
ghar kā sāmān
घर का सामान

fruit and vegetable shop (f)
phal aur sabzī kī dukān
फल और सब्ज़ी की दुकान

car and motorcyle repairs (garage) (m)
gairāj
गैराज

supermarket (m)
suparmārkeṭ
सुपरमार्केट

beauty salon (m)
sailān
सैलॉन

tobacconist (pan shop) (f)
pān kī dukān
पान की दुकान

jeweler (f)
zevrāt kī dukān
ज़ेवरात की दुकान

electronic shop (f)
bijlī kī dukān
बिजली की दुकान

watches and clocks (m) (watch repairer)
gharīsāz
घड़ीसाज़

optician (f)
caśme kī dukān
चश्मे की दुकान

sports store (f)
khelkūd ke sāmān kī dukān
खेलकूद के सामान की दुकान

mobile phone shop (f)
mobāil fon kī dukān
मोबाइल फ़ोन की दुकान

fish shop (f)
machlī kī dukān
मछली की दुकान

sweet shop (f)
miṭhāī kī dukān
मिठाई की दुकान

10.1 Shopping conversations

Where is a … available? (m/f)	***… kahā̃ milegā/milegī?***	… कहाँ मिलेगा/मिलेगी?
At what time does this shop open?	***yeh dukān kitne baje khultī hai?***	यह दुकान कितने बजे खुलती है?
I need/want a …	***mujhe … cāhiye.***	मुझे … चाहिये।
Will you reduce the price?	***kyā āp dām kam kar dẽge?***	क्या आप दाम कम कर देंगे?
Will I get a discount?	***kyā mujhe chūṭ/riyāyat milegī?***	क्या मुझे छूट/रियायत मिलेगी?
I will not pay (give) so much. (m/f)	***maĩ itnā nahī̃ dū̃gā/dū̃gī.***	मैं इतना नहीं दूँगा/दूँगी।
Will you show me some shawls? (m) (polite)	***kyā āp mujhe kuch śāl dikhāẽge?***	क्या आप मुझे कुछ शॉल दिखाएँगे?
Will you show me some shirts? (m)	***kyā āp mujhe kuch kamīzẽ dikhāẽge?***	क्या आप मुझे कुछ कमीज़ें दिखाएँगे?
Does tax also apply?	***kyā śulk bhī lagtā hai?***	क्या शुल्क भी लगता है?
I don't want this.	***mujhe yeh nahī̃ cāhiye.***	मुझे यह नहीं चाहिये।
This is too expensive.	***yeh bahut zyāḍā mahẽgā hai.***	यह बहुत ज़्यादा महँगा है।
I will take this. (m/f)	***maĩ yeh lū̃gā/lū̃gī.***	मैं यह लूँगा/लूँगी।
I will look in one or two more shops. (m/f)	***maĩ ek-do aur dukānõ mẽ dekhū̃gā/dekhū̃gī.***	मैं एक-दो और दुकानों में देखूँगा/देखूँगी।
I will come again. (m/f)	***maĩ phir āū̃gā/āū̃gī.***	मैं फिर आऊँगा/आऊँगी।

What is the price of this?	***is kā dām kyā hai?*** इसका दाम क्या है?
How much is this? (m/f) (of how many)	***yeh kitne kā/kī hai?*** यह कितने का/की है?
Please give me two of these.	***is ke do dījiye.*** इसके दो दीजिये।
I can't pay this much. (m/f)	***maĩ itnā nahī̃ de saktā/saktī.*** मैं इतना नहीं दे सकता/सकती।
Please put it in a bag for me.	***thailī mẽ ḍāliye.*** थैली में डालिये।
We don't have this.	***hamāre pās yeh nahī̃ hai.*** हमारे पास यह नहीं है।
You will get it tomorrow. (m/f) (it be found/ available tomorrow)	***kal milegā/milegī.*** कल मिलेगा/मिलेगी।

paise udhar dījiye. पैसे उधर दीजिये।	Please pay over there.
ham kārḍ se paise nahī̃ lete. हम कार्ड से पैसे नहीं लेते।	We don't accept credit cards.

10.2 Food

Please give me (100 gm) of this.	***is ke (sau grām) dījiye.*** इसके सौ ग्राम दीजिये।
Please put it in a bag for me.	***thailī mẽ ḍāliye.*** थैली में डालिये।
Please give me an assortment (mixed).	***mile-jule dījiye.*** मिले-जुले दीजिये।
Please give me (five) pieces.	***(pā̃c) ṭukṛe dījiye.*** (पाँच) टुकड़े दीजिये।

What is in this? ***is mẽ kyā hai?***
इस में क्या है?

What is in that? ***us mẽ kyā hai?***
उस में क्या है?

Is this sweet? ***kyā yeh mīṭhā hai?***
क्या यह मीठा है?

Is this salty/savory? ***kyā yeh namkīn hai?***
क्या यह नमकीन है?

Is this bitter? ***kyā yeh kaṛvā hai?***
क्या यह कड़वा है?

Is this sour? ***kyā yeh khaṭṭā hai?***
क्या यह खट्टा है?

10.3 Clothing and shoes

shoe/shoes (m)
jūtā/jūte
जूता/जूते

cloth/clothes (m)
kapṛā/kapṛe
कपड़ा/कपड़े

shirt/shirts (f)
kamīz/kamīzẽ
कमीज़/कमीज़ें

shirt/shirts (m)
kurtā/kurte
कुर्ता/कुर्ते

pants (f)
paĩṭ
पैंट

socks (m, pl)
moze
मोज़े

salwar (type of pant) (f)
salvār
सलवार

pyjama (m) (type of pant)
paijāmā
पैजामा

sari/saris (f)
sāṛī/sāṛiyā̃
साड़ी/साड़ियाँ

suit (m)
sūṭ
सूट

shawl (m)
śāl
शॉल

sandals (f)
cappal
चप्पल

scarf (m)
dupaṭṭā
दुपट्टा

raincoat (f)
barsātī
बरसाती

handkerchief (m)
rūmāl
रूमाल

blue
nīlā
नीला

red
lāl
लाल

yellow
pīlā
पीला

orange
nārangī
नारंगी

black
kālā
काला

purple
baiganī
बैगनी

white
safed
सफ़ेद

grey
sleṭī
स्लेटी

green
harā
हरा

brown
bhūrā
भूरा

pink
gulābī
गुलाबी

light color (m)
halkā rang
हल्का रंग

dark color (m)
gehrā rang
गहरा रंग

shiny
camkīlā
चमकीला

golden
sunharā
सुनहरा

durable
ṭikāū
टिकाऊ

dirt-absorbing (doesn't show the dirt)
mailkhor
मैलख़ोर

silk (m)/silk (adj)
reśam/reśmī
रेशम/रेशमी

cotton (f)/cotton (adj)
ruī/sūtī
रुई/सूती

home-spun cotton (f)
khādī
खादी

leather (m)/leather (adj)
camṛā/camṛe kā
चमड़ा/चमड़े का

synthetic (adj)
banāvaṭī
बनावटी

wool (m)/woollen (adj)
ūn/ūnī
ऊन/ऊनी

wood (f)/wooden (adj)
lakṛī/lakṛī kā
लकड़ी/लकड़ी का

real
aslī
असली

fake
naqlī
नक़ली

I would like to see some shirts. (m/f)	***maĩ kuch kamīzẽ dekhnā cāhtā/cāhtī hū̃.*** मैं कुछ कमीज़ें देखना चाहता/चाहती हूँ।
We would like to buy some clothes.	***ham kuch kapṛe kharīdnā cāhte haĩ.*** हम कुछ कपड़े ख़रीदना चाहते हैं।
Do you have a bigger size than this? (m/f)	***kyā āp ke pās is se baṛā/baṛī hai?*** क्या आप के पास इससे बड़ा/बड़ी है?
Do you have a smaller size than this? (m/f)	***kyā āp ke pās is se choṭā/choṭī hai?*** क्या आप के पास इससे छोटा/छोटी है?

Is this genuine?	***kyā yeh aslī hai?*** क्या यह असली है?
This appears fake.	***yeh naqlī dikhtā hai.*** यह नक़ली दिखता है।
Please show me some shawls.	***kuch śāl dikhāiye.*** कुछ शॉल दिखाइये।

hand wash (wash by hand) ***hāth se dhonā*** हाथ से धोना	machine wash ***maśīn mẽ dhonā*** मशीन में धोना

At the cobbler

Will you mend (fix) these shoes? (m) (polite)	***yeh jūte āp ṭhīk kar dẽge?*** ये जूते आप ठीक कर देंगे?
Will you mend (fix) these shoes? (m) (informal)	***yeh jūte tum ṭhīk kar doge?*** ये जूते तुम ठीक कर दोगे?
Will you put a new sole (on them)? (m) (polite) (will you attach a new sole)	***āp nayā talā lagā dẽge?*** आप नया तला लगा देंगे?
Will you put a new sole (on them)? (m) (informal)	***tum nayā talā lagā doge?*** तुम नया तला लगा दोगे?
When should I come?	***maĩ kab āū̃?*** मैं कब आऊँ?
How long will it take to fix them?	***ṭhīk karne mẽ kitnā samay lagegā?*** ठीक करने में कितना समय लगेगा?
Please polish (them). (polite)	***camkā dījiye.*** चमका दीजिये।
Polish (them). (informal)	***camkā do.*** चमका दो।
Please put in new shoe laces. (polite)	***naye fīte lagā dījiye.*** नये फ़ीते लगा दीजिये।

Put in new shoe laces. (informal)	***naye fīte lagā do.*** नये फ़ीते लगा दो।
How much (money) shall I give you?	***kitne paise dū̃?*** कितने पैसे दूँ?

10.4 Cameras

kyā āp ke pās memrī kārḍ haĩ? क्या आपके पास मेमरी कार्ड हैं?	Do you have memory cards?
kyā āp sel becte haĩ? क्या आप सेल बेचते हैं?	Do you sell batteries?
kyā āp merā kaimrā ṭhīk kar sakẽge/sakẽgī? क्या आप मेरा कैमरा ठीक कर सकेंगे/सकेंगी?	Can you fix my camera? (m/f)

It fell.	***yeh gir gayā.*** यह गिर गया।
It broke.	***yeh ṭūṭ gayā.*** यह टूट गया।
This button doesn't work.	***yeh baṭan kām nahī̃ kar rahā hai.*** यह बटन काम नहीं कर रहा है।
The flash doesn't work.	***flaiś kām nahī̃ kar rahī hai.*** फ़्लैश काम नहीं कर रही है।

10.5 At the hairdresser

Do I need an appointment? (is it necessary to take an appointment)	***kyā apāiṇṭmeṇṭ lenā zarūrī hai?*** क्या अपॉइंटमेंट लेना ज़रूरी है?

Please cut my hair. (polite)	***mere bāl kāṭiye*** मेरे बाल काटिये।
Cut my hair. (informal)	***mere bāl kāṭo*** मेरे बाल काटो।
Please cut my hair short. (polite)	***choṭe bāl kāṭiye.*** छोटे बाल काटिये।
Cut my hair short. (informal)	***choṭe bāl kāṭo.*** छोटे बाल काटो।
Please wash my hair. (polite)	***mere bāl dhoiye.*** मेरे बाल धोइये।
Please wash my hair. (informal)	***mere bāl dhoo.*** मेरे बाल धोओ।
Please color my hair. (polite)	***bālõ mẽ rang lagā dījiye.*** बालों में रंग लगा दीजिये।
Color my hair. (informal)	***bālõ mẽ rang lagā do.*** बालों में रंग लगा दो।
Please shave my beard. (polite)	***dāṛhī banāiye.*** दाढ़ी बनाइये।
Shave my beard. (informal)	***dāṛhī banāo.*** दाढ़ी बनाओ।
Please shave my moustache. (polite)	***mũchẽ banāiye.*** मूँछें बनाइये।
Shave my moustache. (informal)	***mũchẽ banāo.*** मूँछें बनाओ।
Please give (me) a massage. (polite)	***māliś kar dījiye.*** मालिश कर दीजिये।
Give (me) a massage. (informal)	***māliś kar do.*** मालिश कर दो।
Please (don't) use oil. (polite)	***tel kā istemāl (mat) kījiye.*** तेल का इस्तेमाल (मत) कीजिये।
Please (don't) use oil. (informal)	***tel kā istemāl (mat) karo.*** तेल का इस्तेमाल (मत) करो।

11 Tourist Activities

11. Tourist Activities

11.1 Places of interest

● **There are** many places of religious, historical, and cultural interest throughout India. In large cities like New Delhi, there will be a tourist office where you can obtain information. There is also often a tourist reservation office at major railway stations, and a tourist quota on select trains.

Do you know where the tourist office is?	***kyā āpko mālūm hai ki ṭūrisṭ āfis kahā̃ hai?*** क्या आपको मालूम है कि टूरिस्ट ऑफ़िस कहाँ है?
Can I get a map of the city? (is a map available/found)	***kyā śehar kā naqśā milegā?*** क्या शहर का नक़्शा मिलेगा?
Where is the (Red Fort)?	***(lāl qilā) kahā̃ hai?*** (लाल क़िला) कहाँ है?
What is worth seeing in … ?	***… mẽ kyā dekhne lāyaq hai?*** … में क्या देखने लायक़ है?
What's the easiest way to get to …?	***… jāne kā sab se āsān rāstā kyā hai?*** … जाने का सब से आसान रास्ता क्या है?
Do you have some information about…? (will some information be available)	***… kī kuch jānkārī milegī?*** … की कुछ जानकारी मिलेगी?
Will you show me on the map? (m/f)	***kyā āp naqśe mẽ dikhāẽge/ dikhāẽgī?*** क्या आप नक़्शे में दिखाएँगे/ दिखाएँगी?

What are the most important historical sites here?	***yahā̃ sab se aham aitihāsik sthān kyā haĩ?*** यहाँ सब से अहम ऐतिहासिक स्थान क्या हैं?
What are the most important religious sites here?	***yahā̃ sab se aham dhārmik sthal kyā haĩ?*** यहाँ सब से अहम धार्मिक स्थल क्या हैं?
Are these Hindu temples?	***kyā ye hinduõ ke mandir haĩ?*** क्या ये हिन्दुओं के मंदिर हैं?
Are these Buddhist temples?	***kyā ye bauddh mandir haĩ?*** क्या ये बौद्ध मंदिर हैं?
Where is the museum?	***sangrahālay kahā̃ hai?*** संग्रहालय कहाँ है?
What should I see here?	***yahā̃ kyā dekhū̃?*** यहाँ क्या देखूँ?
What should we see here?	***yahā̃ kyā dekhẽ?*** यहाँ क्या देखें?
We will stay here for one day.	***ham yahā̃ ek din rukẽge.*** हम यहाँ एक दिन रुकेंगे।
We will stay here for three days.	***ham yahā̃ tīn din rukẽge.*** हम यहाँ तीन दिन रुकेंगे।
We will stay here for one week.	***ham yahā̃ ek hafte rukẽge.*** हम यहाँ एक हफ़्ते रुकेंगे।
We will stay here for two weeks.	***ham yahā̃ do hafte rukẽge.*** हम यहाँ दो हफ़्ते रुकेंगे।

fort (m) ***qilā*** क़िला	temple (m) ***mandir*** मंदिर	gurudwara (m) ***gurudwārā*** गुरुद्वारा
mosque (f) ***masjid*** मस्जिद	church (m) ***kalīsā/girjā*** कलीसा/गिरजा	Jain temple (m) ***jain mandir*** जैन मंदिर

park (m) ***pārk*** पार्क	new city (m) ***nayā śehar*** नया शहर	ocean (m) ***samudra*** समुद्र
garden (m) ***baghīcā*** बग़ीचा	old city (m) ***purānā śehar*** पुराना शहर	metro station (m) ***meṭro sṭeśan*** मेट्रो स्टेशन
museum (m) ***sangrahālay*** संग्रहालय	cinema hall (m) ***sinemāhāl*** सिनेमाहाल	mausoleum (m) ***maqbarā*** मक़बरा
statue (f) ***mūrti*** मूर्ति	pond (m) ***tālāb*** तालाब	graveyard (m) ***qabristān*** क़ब्रिस्तान

How long does it take to get there?
jāne mẽ kitnī der lagtī hai?
जाने में कितनी देर लगती है।

Where do we catch it?
ise kahā̃ se pakaṛte haĩ?
इसे कहाँ से पकड़ते हैं?

Can we take a city tour?
siṭī ṭūr par jā sakte haĩ?
सिटी टूर पर जा सकते हैं?

From where does the bus depart?
bas kahā̃ se jātī hai?
बस कहाँ से जाती है?

Can we hire a guide? (will a guide be found)
kyā gāiḍ milegā?
क्या गाइड मिलेगा?

How much should we pay him/her?
use kitne paise dene cāhiye?
उसे कितने पैसे देने चाहिये?

Can we go on a tour there?
kyā vahā̃ ham ṭūr par jā sakẽge?
क्या वहाँ हम टूर पर जा सकेंगे?

For how many days should we stay there?
ham vahā̃ kitne din rehẽ?
हम वहाँ कितने दिन रहें?

Can we go for a stoll?
ham ṭehalne ke liye jā sakẽge?
हम टहलने के लिये जा सकेंगे?

When does it open? (m/f)
voh kitne baje khultā/khultī hai?
वह कितने बजे खुलता/खुलती है?

What time does it close? (m/f)	***voh kitne baje band hotā/hotī hai?*** वह कितने बजे बंद होता/होती है?
Does it open seven days a week? (m/f)	***kyā yeh hafte mẽ sāt din khultā/khultī hai?*** क्या यह हफ़्ते में सात दिन खुलता/खुलती है?
Do seniors get a discount?	***kyā buzurgõ ko chūṭ miltī hai?*** क्या बुज़ुर्गों को छूट मिलती है?
What is the admission price?	***andar jāne kā ṭikaṭ kitne kā hai?*** अंदर जाने का टिकट कितने का है?
May I take photos here?	***kyā maĩ yahā̃ tasvīr khī̃c saktā/saktī hū̃?*** क्या मैं यहाँ तस्वीर खींच सकता/सकती हूँ?
Do you have postcards?	***kyā āpke pās posṭkārḍ haĩ?*** क्या आप के पास पोस्टकार्ड हैं?
Do you have a brochure?	***kyā āpke pās brośar hai?*** क्या आप के पास ब्रोशर है?

11.2 Going out

● **Going out** in India depends very much on the city you are visiting. Larger cities have a lot of attractions, including cultural shows, movies, live theater, cultural and historical sites, festivals and many restaurants with a tremendous variety of cuisine. In cities like Bombay and Delhi, there is always something going on, and several guides to the week's events, including the very popular *Delhi Diary*, *TimeOut Delhi* and *TimeOut Bombay* (the latter two are also online guides) in Delhi, are available.

Do you have a copy of …?	***kyā āp ke pās … kī kāpī hai?*** क्या आपके पास ... की कॉपी है?

Is there anything on this evening?	***kyā āj śām ko kuch honevālā hai?*** क्या आज शाम को कुछ होनेवाला है?
We want to see	***ham ... dekhnā cāhte haĩ.*** हम ... देखना चाहते हैं।
What is on at the cinema?	***sinemāhāl mẽ kyā lagā hai?*** सिनेमाहाल में क्या लगा है?
Is this a good movie?	***kyā yeh acchī film hai?*** क्या यह अच्छी फ़िल्म है?
What times are the shows?	***śo kitne baje hote haĩ?*** शो कितने बजे होते हैं?
Is there a (6 o'clock) show?	***kyā (chai baje) kā śo hai?*** क्या (छै बजे का) शो है?
Is there a (9 o'clock) show?	***kyā (nau baje) kā śo hai?*** क्या (नौ बजे का) शो है?
What is the best restaurant here?	***yahā̃ sab se acchā restrā̃ kaunsā hai?*** यहाँ सब से अच्छा रेस्त्राँ कौनसा है?
Is this an expensive restaurant?	***kyā yeh bahut mahẽgā restrā̃ hai?*** क्या यह बहुत महँगा रेस्त्राँ है?
What sort of cuisine is it? (what sort of food is available)	***kaisā khānā miltā hai?*** कैसा खाना मिलता है?
Should we wear good clothes? (having worn good clothes go)	***kyā acche kapṛe pehan kar jānā cāhiye?*** क्या अच्छे कपड़े पहनकर जाना चाहिये?
Is there a cricket match on? (happening)	***kyā krikeṭ kā maic ho rahā hai?*** क्या क्रिकेट का मैच हो रहा है?
Who is playing?	***kaun khel rahā hai?*** कौन खेल रहा है?
Are tickets available?	***kyā ṭikaṭ milẽge?*** क्या टिकट मिलेंगे?

11.3 Booking tickets

Where is the booking office?	***buking āfis kahā̃ hai?*** बुकिंग ऑफ़िस कहाँ है?
How much are the tickets?	***ṭikaṭ kitne ke haĩ?*** टिकट कितने के हैं?
Should we buy the tickets now?	***kyā abhī ṭikaṭ kharīdne cāhiye?*** क्या अभी टिकट ख़रीदने चाहिये?
Can I have tickets in the balcony? (are balcony tickets available)	***bālkanī ke ṭikaṭ milẽge?*** बालकनी के टिकट मिलेंगे?

12 Sports Activities

12. Sports Activities

12.1 Sporting questions

Where can we hire a ...? (m/f)	***... kirāye par kahā̃ milegā/milegī?*** ... किराये पर कहाँ मिलेगा/मिलेगी?
Is there any sports store here?	***kyā yahā̃ khel-kūd ke sāmān kī dukān hai?*** क्या यहाँ खेल-कूद के सामान की दुकान है?
Is there anywhere to play cricket? (a place somewhere to play cricket)	***kyā kahī̃ kriket khelne kī jagah hai?*** क्या कहीं क्रिकेट खेलने की जगह है?
Is there a pool anywhere around here?	***kyā yahā̃ ke āspās pūl hai?*** क्या यहाँ के आसपास पूल है?
Do I have to become a member? (is it necessary to become a member)	***kyā membar bannā zarūrī hai?*** क्या मेम्बर बनना ज़रूरी है?
How much is this?	***yeh kitne kā hai?*** यह कितने का है?
Do I need a permit?	***kyā mujhe parmiṭ cāhiye?*** क्या मुझे परमिट चाहिये?
Where is a permit available?	***parmiṭ kahā̃ milegā?*** परमिट कहाँ मिलेगा?

12.2 By the waterfront

Can I swim in this water?	***kyā is pānī mẽ maĩ tair saktā/saktī hū̃?*** क्या इस पानी में मैं तैर सकता/सकती हूँ?
Is there a swimming pool around here?	***kyā yahā̃ ke āspās pūl hai?*** क्या यहाँ के आसपास पूल है?
Is the water clean?	***kyā pānī sāf hai?*** क्या पानी साफ़ है?

13 Health Matters

13. Health Matters

13.1 Calling a doctor

● **If you become ill** or need emergency treatment, it is best to go straight to a doctor, or to the nearest hospital. The quality of hospitals can vary in both large cities and smaller centers. It is best to find out in advance which hospitals are highly regarded by local residents.

I am sick.	***maĩ bīmār hũ.*** मैं बीमार हूँ।
I need a doctor. (the necessity of a doctor)	***mujhe ḍākṭar kī zarūrat hai.*** मुझे डॉक्टर की ज़रूरत है?
Please call/summon a doctor.	***ḍākṭar ko bulāiye.*** डॉक्टर को बुलाइये।
I need to go to hospital.	***mujhe aspatāl jānā cāhiye.*** मुझे अस्पताल जाना चाहिये।
When will the doctor come?	***ḍākṭar kab āegā?*** डॉक्टर कब आएगा?
I need to see a doctor. (I have to show a doctor)	***ḍākṭar ko dikhānā hai.*** डॉक्टर को दिखाना है।
Do I need an appointment?	***kyā apāiṇṭmeṇṭ cāhiye?*** क्या अपॉइंटमेंट चाहिये?
I feel very sick. (m/f)	***maĩ bahut bīmār ho gayā/gayī hũ.*** मैं बहुत बीमार हो गया/गयी हूँ।
Please take me to the hospital. (polite)	***mujhe aspatāl le jāiye.*** मुझे अस्पताल ले जाइये।

13.2 What's wrong?

I don't feel well. (my health is not okay)	***merī tabiyat ṭhīk nahī̃ hai.*** मेरी तबियत ठीक नहीं है।
My friend is sick. (m/f)	***mere/merī dost kī tabiyat ṭhīk nahī̃ hai.*** मेरे/मेरी दोस्त की तबियत ठीक नहीं है।
I am dizzy.	***cakkar ā rahā hai.*** चक्कर आ रहा है।
I feel like vomiting.	***ulṭī hone kā ehsās ho rahā hai.*** उल्टी होने का एहसास हो रहा है।
I was vomiting.	***ulṭī ho rahī thī.*** उल्टी हो रही थी।
I have a cold.	***zukām hai.*** ज़ुकाम है।
I have pain right here.	***yahī̃ dard hai.*** यहीं दर्द है।
I have a stomach ache. (there is pain in the stomach)	***peṭ mẽ dard hai.*** पेट में दर्द है।
I have a fever.	***bukhār hai.*** बुख़ार है।
I was bitten by a dog.	***ek kutte ne mujhe kāṭā.*** एक कुत्ते ने मुझे काटा।
I was bitten by a monkey.	***ek bandar ne mujhe kāṭā.*** एक बंदर ने मुझे काटा।
I have a headache.	***sardard hai.*** सरदर्द है।
I fell over. (m/f)	***maĩ gir gayā/gayī.*** मैं गिर गया/गयी।
I sprained my (ankle).	***(ṭakhne mẽ) moc ā gayī.*** (टख़ने में) मोच आ गयी।

I burned my skin.	***merī khāl jal gayī.*** मेरी खाल जल गयी।
Perhaps I am pregnant.	***śāyad maĩ garbhvatī hū̃.*** शायद मैं गर्भवती हूँ।

13.3 The consultation

kyā huā? क्या हुआ?	What happened?
kyā ho rahā hai? क्या हो रहा है?	What is happening?
yeh dard kab se ho rahā hai? यह दर्द कब से हो रहा है?	How long have you had this pain?
yeh kabhī pehle huā hai? यह कभी पहले हुआ है?	Has this happened before?
kamīz utāriye. कमीज़ उतारिये।	Please take off your shirt.
yahā̃ leṭiye. यहाँ लेटिये।	Please lie down here.
kyā yahā̃ dard hai? क्या यहाँ दर्द है?	Is there pain here?
gehrī sā̃s lījiye. गहरी साँस लीजिये।	Take a deep breath.
sā̃s choṛiye. साँस छोड़िये।	Breathe out.
mū̃h kholiye. मुँह खोलिये।	Open your mouth.

Patient's medical history

I have diabetes.	***madhumeh kī bīmārī hai.*** मधुमेह की बीमारी है।

I have a heart condition.	***dil kī bīmārī hai.*** दिल की बीमारी है।
I have asthma.	***damā hai.*** दमा है।
I am allergic to….	***… kī elarjī hai.*** … की एलर्जी है।
I am pregnant.	***maĩ garbhvatī hū̃.*** मैं गर्भवती हूँ।
I am pregnant. (I am about to become a mother)	***maĩ mā̃ bannevālī hū̃.*** मैं माँ बननेवाली हूँ।
I am (six months) pregnant.	***merā (chai mahīne) kā garbh hai.*** मेरा (छै महीने) का गर्भ है।
I am on a diet. (m)	***maĩ ḍāiṭing kar rahā hū̃.*** मैं डाइटिंग कर रहा हूँ।
I am on a diet. (f)	***maĩ ḍāiṭing kar rahī hū̃.*** मैं डाइटिंग कर रही हूँ।
I am taking medication/ medicine. (m)	***maĩ davā khā rahā hū̃.*** मैं दवा खा रहा हूँ।
I am taking medication/ medicine. (f)	***maĩ davā khā rahī hū̃.*** मैं दवा खा रही हूँ।
This is my medication/ medicine.	***yeh merī davā hai.*** यह मेरी दवा है।
I take this daily. (m/f)	***maĩ yeh roz khātā/khātī hū̃.*** मैं यह रोज़ खाता/खाती हूँ।
I have had a heart attack.	***dil kā daurā paṛ cukā hai.*** दिल का दौरा पड़ चुका है।
I have been ill for a while.	***maĩ kāfī samay se bīmār hū̃.*** मैं काफी समय से बीमार हूँ।
I have a stomach ulcer.	***peṭ mẽ alsar hai.*** पेट में अलसर है।
I have my period (menstruation).	***māsik dharm ho rahā hai.*** मासिकधर्म हो रहा है।

Do you have any allergies.	***kisī cīz kī elarjī hai?*** किसी चीज़ की एलर्जी है?
Are you taking any medication? (m)	***koī davā khā rahe haĩ?*** कोई दवा खा रहे हैं?
Are you taking any medication? (f)	***koī davā khā rahe haĩ?*** कोई दवा खा रही हैं?
Are you pregnant?	***kyā āp garbhvatī haĩ?*** क्या आप गर्भवती हैं?
Have you had a tetanus injection? (has an injection been applied)	***ṭeṭnas kī suī lagvāī?*** टेटनस की सुई लगवाई?

The diagnosis

gabhīr māmlā nahī̃ hai. गंभीर मामला नहीं है।	It is nothing serious. (not a serious issue)
āpkā … ṭūṭ gayā hai. आपका ... टूट गया है।	Your … is broken. (m)
āpkī … ṭūṭ gayī hai. आपकी ... टूट गयी है।	Your … is broken. (f)
āpke … mẽ moc ā gayī hai. आपके ... में मोच आ गयी है।	You have a sprained … (m)
āpkī … mẽ moc ā gayī hai. आपकी ... में मोच आ गयी है।	You have a sprained … (f)
infekśan hai. इन्फ़ेक्शन है।	You have an infection.
apeṇḍisāiṭis hai. अपेंडिसाइटिस है।	You have appendicitis.
āpko bukhār hai. आपको बुख़ार है।	You have a fever.
gupt rog hai. गुप्त रोग है।	You have an STD.

āpko flū ho gayā hai. आपको फ़्लू हो गया है।	You have the flu.
dil kā daurā huā hai. दिल का दौरा हुआ है।	You have had a heart attack.
āpko infekśan ho gayā hai. आपको इन्फ़ेक्शन हो गया है।	You have a (bacterial) infection.
āpko nimoniyā ho gayā hai. आपको निमोनिया हो गया है।	You have pneumonia.
āpko alsar ho gayā hai. आपको अलसर हो गया है।	You have an ulcer.
mānspeśī khĩc gayī hai. मांसपेशी खिंच गयी है।	You've pulled a muscle. (a muscle has been pulled)
āpko fūḍ pāizaning huā hai. आपको फ़ूड पाइज़निंग हुआ है।	You have food poisoning.
āpko lū lagī hai. आपको लू लगी है।	You have sunstroke. (a hot wind wind has attached)
āpko … kī elarjī ho gayī hai. आपको … की एलर्जी हो गयी है।	You have an allergy to …
āp mā̃ bannevālī haĩ. आप माँ बननेवाली हैं।	You are pregnant. (you are about to become a mother)
kh̲ūn kī jā̃c hogī. ख़ून की जाँच होगी।	Your blood will be tested.
peśāb kī jā̃c hogī. पेशाब की जाँच होगी।	Your urine will be tested.
ṭaṭṭī kī jā̃c hogī. टट्टी की जाँच होगी।	Your stool will be tested.
āpkā āpareśan honā cāhiye. आपका आपरेशन होना चाहिये।	You will need an operation.

Is this disease contagious? ***kyā yeh rog sankrāmak hai?*** क्या यह रोग संक्रामक है?

How long should I stay in bed? ***mujhe kitne din palang par rehnā cāhiye?*** मुझे कितने दिन पलंग पर रहना चाहिये?

How long will I stay in hospital? (m/f)	***maĩ aspatāl mẽ kitne din rahū̃gā/rahū̃gī?*** मैं अस्पताल में कितने दिन रहूँगा/रहूँगी?
Should I stay away from some foods?	***mujhe khāne mẽ parhez karnā cāhiye?*** मुझे खाने में परहेज़ करना चाहिये?
Can I travel? (m/f)	***kyā maĩ yātrā kar saktā/saktī hū̃?*** क्या मैं यात्रा कर सकता/सकती हूँ?
When should I come back?	***mujhe kab vāpas ānā cāhiye?*** मुझे कब वापस आना चाहिये?
I will come again tomorrow. (m/f)	***maĩ kal phir āū̃gā/āū̃gī.*** मैं कल फिर आऊँगा/आऊँगी।
How many times a day do I take this medicine?	***din mẽ kitnī bār mujhe yeh davā khānī cāhiye?*** दिन में कितनी बार मुझे यह दवा खानी चाहिये?

13.4 Medications and prescriptions

How many pills each time?	***har bār kitnī goliyā̃ khānī cāhiye?*** हर बार कितनी गोलियाँ खानी चाहिये?
How many times a day?	***roz kitnī bār?*** रोज़ कितनी बार?
I've forgot to bring my medication. (m/f)	***davā lānā bhūl gayā/gayī.*** दवा लाना भूल गया/गयी।
At home I take … (m/f)	***ghar par maĩ … letā/letī hū̃.*** घर पर मैं ... लेता/लेती हूँ।

Could you write a prescription for me?	***kyā āp mere liye davā kā nuskhā likhẽge/likhẽgī?*** क्या आप मेरे लिये दवा का नुस्ख़ा लिखेंगे/लिखेंगी?
I am giving you antibiotics. (m)	***maĩ āpko eṇṭībāyoṭik de rahā hū̃.*** मैं आपको एंटीबायोटिक दे रहा हूँ।
I am giving you antibiotics. (f)	***maĩ āpko eṇṭībāyoṭik de rahī hū̃.*** मैं आपको एंटीबायोटिक दे रही हूँ।

Stay in bed.
palang par rahiye.
पलंग पर रहिये।

Don't go outside.
bāhar na jāiye.
बाहर न जाइये।

pills/tablets
goliyā̃.
गोलियाँ

finish the prescription
kors pūrā karnā cāhiye.
कोर्स पूरा करना चाहिये।

spoonful
bharā huā cammac
भरा हुआ चम्मच

dissolve in water
pānī mẽ gholnā
पानी में घोलना

swallow
nigalnā
निगलना

injection (f)
suī
सुई

drops (f)
bū̃ndẽ
बूँदें

after every ... hours
har ... ghaṇṭe bād
हर ... घंटे बाद

ointment
marham
मरहम

take (eat)
khānā
खाना

for ... days
... dinõ ke liye
... दिनों के लिये

before meals
khāne se pehle
खाने से पहले

after eating
khāne ke bād
खाने के बाद

rub on
lagānā
लगाना

... times a day
din mẽ ... bār
दिन में ... बार

14 Emergencies

14. Emergencies

14.1 Asking for help

Help!	***bacāo!*** बचाओ!
Fire!	***āg lag gayī!*** आग लग गयी!
Police!	***pulis!*** पुलिस!
Quick/hurry!	***jaldī!*** जल्दी!
Danger!	***khatrā!*** ख़तरा!
Stop!	***ṭhehro!*** ठहरो!
Be careful!/Go easy! (with vigilance)	***sāvadhānī se!*** सावधानी से!
Don't put your hands on me!	***hāth mat lagāo!*** हाथ मत लगाओ!
Let go! (leave)	***choṛo!*** छोड़ो!
Stop thief! (catch the thief)	***cor ko pakṛo!*** चोर को पकड़ो!
Please help me.	***merī madad kījiye.*** मेरी मदद कीजिये।

āg bujhāne kā sādhan kahā̃ hai?
आग बुझाने का साधन कहाँ है? Where's the nearest fire extinguisher?

pulis kā thānā kahā̃ hai? पुलिस का थाना कहाँ है?	Where's the police station?
damkal ke logõ ko bulāo! दमकल के लोगों को बुलाओ!	Call the fire department!
puils ko bulāo! पुलिस को बुलाओ!	Call the police!
embulens ko bulāo! एम्बुलेंस को बुलाओ!	Call an ambulance!

Where's a phone?	***fon kahā̃ hai?*** फ़ोन कहाँ है?
May I use your phone?	***maĩ āpke fon kā istemāl karū̃?*** मैं आपके फोन का इस्तेमाल करूँ?
What's the emergency number?	***āpatkāl kā nambar kyā hai?*** आपत्काल का नम्बर क्या है?
What's the number for the police?	***pulis kā nambar kyā hai?*** पुलिस का नम्बर क्या है?

14.2 Lost items

I've lost my wallet. (my wallet is lost)	***merā baṭuā kho gayā.*** मेरा बटुआ खो गया।
I lost my … here yesterday. (m/f)	***kal yahā̃ merā/merī … kho gayā/gayī.*** कल मेरा/मेरी … खो गया/गयी।
I left my … here. (m/f)	***maĩ apnā/apnī … yahā̃ choṛ gayā/gayī.*** मैं अपना/अपनी … यहाँ छोड़ गया/गयी।
Did you find my …? (m/f)	***āpko merā/merī … milā/milī?*** आपको मेरा/मेरी … मिला/मिली?
It was right here. (m/f)	***yahī̃ thā/thī.*** यहीं था/थी।

It is a very valuable thing.	***bahut beśqīmtī cīz hai.*** बहुत बेशक़ीमती चीज़ है।
Where is the lost and found office? (where do you keep lost things)	***khoī huī cīzẽ kahā̃ rakhte haĩ?*** खोई हुई चीज़ें कहाँ रखते हैं?

14.3 Accidents

There's been an accident.	***durghaṭnā huī hai.*** दुर्घटना हुई है।
Someone's fallen into the water.	***koī pānī mẽ gir gayā hai.*** कोई पानी में गिर गया है।
There's a fire.	***āg lag gayī hai.*** आग लग गयी है।
Is anyone hurt? (an injury attached to anyone)	***kisī ko coṭ lagī?*** किसी को चोट लगी?
Nobody/somone has been injured.	***kisī ko coṭ (nahī̃) lagī.*** किसी को चोट (नहीं) लगी।
Someone is still trapped in the car/vehicle.	***koī gāṛī mẽ phā̃sā huā hai.*** कोई गाड़ी में फँसा हुआ है।
It's not too bad.	***itnā kharāb nahī̃ hai.*** इतना ख़राब नहीं है।
Don't worry.	***cintā na kījiye.*** चिन्ता न कीजिये।
Don't touch anything.	***kisī cīz ko mat chuo.*** किसी चीज़ को मत छुओ।
I want to talk to the police first. (m/f)	***pehle maĩ pulis se bāt karnā cahtā/cāhtī hū̃.*** पहले मैं पुलिस से बात करना चाहता/चाहती हूँ।

I want to take a photo first. (m/f)	***pehle maĩ foṭo khĩcnā cāhtā/ cāhtī hũ.*** पहले मैं फ़ोटो खींचना चाहता/चाहती हूँ।
Here's my name and address.	***yeh merā nām aur patā hai.*** यह मेरा नाम और पता है।
May I have (know) your name and address?	***apnā nām aur patā batāiye.*** अपना नाम और पता बताइये।

apnā lāisens dikhāiye. अपना लाइसेंस दिखाइये।	Could I see your license?
kyā āp gavāh banẽge/banẽgī? क्या आप गवाह बनेंगे/बनेंगी?	Will you act as a witness? (m/f)
mujhe yeh jānkārī bīme ke liye cāhiye. मुझे यह जानकारी बीमे के लिये चाहिये।	I need this information for the insurance.
bīmā hai? बीमा है?	Are you insured? (is there insurance)
yahā̃ hastākṣar kījiye. यहाँ हस्ताक्षर कीजिये।	Please sign here.

14.4 Theft

I have been robbed. (a robbery has happened)	***corī huī hai.*** चोरी हुई है।
My … has been stolen. (m/f)	***merā/merī … corī ho gayā/gayī.*** मेरा/मेरी … चोरी हो गया/गयी।
My car has been broken into. (from the car a robbery has happened)	***gāṛī se corī huī hai.*** गाड़ी से चोरी हुई है।

14.5 Missing person

My child/grandmother has disappeared. (m/f)	***merā baccā/merī dādī <u>gh</u>āyab ho gayā/gayī.***	मेरा बच्चा/मेरी दादी ग़ायब हो गया/गयी।
Will you search with me? (m/f)	***āp mere sāth talāś karẽge/karẽgī?***	आप मेरे साथ तलाश करेंगे/करेंगी?
Have you seen a small child? (m)	***āpne ek choṭe bacce ko dekhā?***	आपने एक छोटे बच्चे को देखा?
Have you seen a small child? (f)	***āpne ek choṭī baccī ko dekhā?***	आपने एक छोटी बच्ची को देखा?
He's/she's … years old? (m/f)	***voh … sāl kā/kī hai.***	वह … साल का/की है।
His/her hair is long.	***us ke bāl lambe haĩ.***	उसके बाल लम्बे हैं।
His/her hair is short.	***us ke bāl choṭe haĩ.***	उसके बाल छोटे हैं।
He/She is fair (Caucasian). (m/f)	***voh gorā/gorī hai.***	वह गोरा/गोरी है।
He/she was wearing a …	***voh … pehne hai.***	वह … पहने है।
a sweater (m)	***sveṭar***	स्वेटर
a coat (m)	***koṭ***	कोट
a t-shirt (f)	***ṭī śarṭ***	टी शर्ट
a dress (f)	***ḍres***	ड्रेस
He/she has glasses. (glasses are attached)	***caśmā pehane hue hai.***	चश्मा पहने हुए है।

This is his/her photo.	***yeh uskī tasvīr hai.*** यह उसकी तस्वीर है।
He must be lost.	***voh kho gayā hogā.*** वह खो गया होगा।
She must be lost.	***voh kho gayī hogī.*** वह खो गयी होगी।

14.6 The police

An arrest

mujhe hindī nahī̃ ātī. मुझे हिन्दी नहीं आती।	I don't speak Hindi.
lāisens dikhāiye. लाइसेंस दिखाइये।	Please show me your license.
āp bahut tez gati se calā rahe the. आप बहुत तेज़ गति से चला रहे थे।	You were speeding. (m)
āp bahut tez gati se calā rahī thī̃. आप बहुत तेज़ गति से चला रही थीं।	You were speeding. (f)
āp yahā̃ gāṛī lagā nahī̃ sakte/saktī̃. आप यहाँ गाड़ी लगा नहीं सकते/सकतीं।	You can't park here. (m/f)
gāṛī kī battiyā̃ kām nahī̃ kar rahī haĩ. गाड़ी की बत्तियाँ काम नहीं कर रही हैं।	The car's lights are not working.
āpko jurmānā denā paṛegā. आपको जुर्माना देना पड़ेगा।	You'll have to pay a fine.
āp abhī de sakte/saktī haĩ. आप अभी दे सकते/सकती हैं।	You can pay now. (m/f)

I didn't see the sign. (the sign was not visible)	***sāin dikhāī nahī̃ diyā.*** साइन दिखाई नहीं दिया।
I don't understand this.	***yeh merī samajh mẽ nahī̃ ātā.*** यह मेरी समझ में नहीं आता।
I was only going ... kms an hour. (m)	***maĩ sirf ... kilomīṭar kī gati se calā rahā thā.*** मैं सिर्फ़ ... किलोमीटर की गति से चला रहा था।
I was only going ... kms an hour. (f)	***maĩ sirf ... kilomīṭar kī gati se calā rahī thī.*** मैं सिर्फ़ ... किलोमीटर की गति से चला रही थी।
I will have the car checked. (m/f)	***gāṛī kī sarvisiṅg karāū̃gā/karāū̃gī.*** गाड़ी की सर्विसिंग कराऊँगा/कराऊँगी।
I couldn't see because of the lights.	***tez rośnī kī vajah se kuch dikhāī nahī̃ de rahā thā.*** तेज़ रोशनी की वजह से कुछ दिखाई नहीं दे रहा था।

āī. ḍī. kārḍ dikhāiye. आई० डी० कार्ड दिखाइये।	Please show me your I.D. card.
kitne baje huā? कितने बजे हुआ?	What time did it happen?
kyā koī gavāh hai? क्या कोई गवाह है?	Is there a witness?
yahā̃ hastākṣar kījiye. यहाँ हस्ताक्षर कीजिये।	Sign here, please.
āpko angrezī bolnevālā cāhiye? आपको अंग्रेज़ी बोलनेवाला चाहिये?	Do you want an interpreter? (English speaker)

At the police station

I want to report a collision/rape. (m/f)	***maĩ durghaṭnā/balātkār kī riporṭ darj karānā cāhtā/cāhtī hū̃.***	मैं दुर्घटना/बलात्कार की रिपोर्ट दर्ज कराना चाहता/चाहती हूँ।
Please make a statement.	***bayān dījiye.***	बयान दीजिये।
Please give me a copy for insurance.	***bīme ke liye mujhe ek kāpī dījiye.***	बीमे के लिये एक कॉपी दीजिये।
I have lost everything.	***sab kuch kho gayā hai.***	सब कुछ खो गया है।
I've no money left. (m/f)	***mere pās kuch bhī paise nahī̃ haĩ.***	मेरे पास कुछ भी पैसे नहीं हैं।
Can you give me a little money?	***āp mujhe thoṛe se paise de sakẽge/ sakẽgī?***	आप मुझे थोड़े से पैसे दे सकेंगे/सकेंगी?
I need an interpreter.	***mujhe angrezī bolnevālā cāhiye.***	मुझे अंग्रेज़ी बोलनेवाला चाहिये।
I am innocent.	***maĩ nirdoṣ hū̃.***	मैं निर्दोष हूँ।
I don't know anything about this.	***is bare mẽ mujhe kuch mālūm nahī̃ hai.***	इस बारे में मुझे कुछ मालूम नहीं है।
I want to speak to someone from my embassy. (m/f)	***maĩ apne deś ke dūtāvas ke logõ se bāt karnā cāhtā/cāhtī hū̃.***	मैं अपने देश के दूतावास के लोगों से बात करना चाहता/चाहती हूँ।
I want an English-speaking lawyer.	***mujhe angrezī bolnevāle vakīl cāhiye.***	मुझे अंग्रेज़ी बोलनेवाले वकील चाहिये।

15 Religion

15. Religion

15.1 Religion in India

• **The vast majority** of people in India identify themselves as Hindus, although this means vastly different things to different people in various parts of the country. In addition to Hinduism, the largest minority population in India is Muslim, with much smaller minorities of Sikhs, Christians and Jains, Zoroastrians, Buddhists and Jews. Within Hinduism there are many different sects, local deities, beliefs and practices. There are also many Hindus (and people of other faiths, of course), for whom religion does not play a very large part in their day-to-day lives. It can be overwhelming for the first-time visitor to India. However, people are generally extremely happy to explain their own faith and religious practices if politely asked. It is always best to be respectful at places of religious worship, and the best way is to be as unintrusive as possible. There are one or two religious sites that are open only to people of that faith.

Hindu (m)
hindū
हिंदू

Hinduism (m)
hindū dharm
हिंदू धर्म

Muslim (m)
musalmān/muslim
मुसलमान/मुसलिम

Islam (m)
islām
इसलाम

Christian
īsāī
ईसाई

Christianity (m)
īsāī dharm
ईसाई धर्म

Buddhist (m)
bauddh dharm kā anuyāyī
बौद्ध धर्म का अनुयायी

Buddhism (m)
bauddh dharm
बौद्ध धर्म

Jewish
yahūdī
यहूदी

Judaism (m)
yahūdī dharm
यहूदी धर्म

Sikh (m)
sikkh
सिक्ख

Sikhism (m)
sikkh dharm
सिक्ख धर्म

temple (m)
mandir
मंदिर

mosque (f)
masjid
मस्जिद

gurudwara (Sikh temple) (m)
gurudvāra
गुरुद्वारा

religion (for Hindus and others) (m)
dharm
धर्म

religion (for Muslims) (m)
mazhab
मज़हब

Sunni (one of the two major sects of Islam)
sunnī
सुन्नी

Shia (one of the two major sects of Islam)
śiyā
शिया

God (for Hindus) (m)
īśvar/bhagvān
ईश्वर/भगवान

God (for Muslims) (m)
allāh/khudā
अल्लाह/ख़ुदा

God (for Christians) (m)
prabhu/īśvar
प्रभु/ईश्वर

Jesus Christ
īsā masīh
ईसा मसीह

God (for Sikhs) (m)
rab
रब

fast (for Hindus) (m)
vrat
व्रत

fast (for Muslims) (m)
rozā
रोज़ा

prayer (for Hindus) (f)
prārthnā
प्रार्थना

prayer (for Christians) (f)
prārthnā
प्रार्थना

prayer (formal) (for Muslims) (f)
namāz
नमाज़

prayer (for Muslims) (f)
duā
दुआ

āp īsāī haĩ? आप ईसाई हैं?	Are you Christian?
āp hindū haĩ? आप हिंदू हैं?	Are you Hindu?
kyā āp āstik haĩ? क्या आप आस्तिक हैं?	Do you believe in God? (m/f)
maĩ nāstik hũ मैं नास्तिक हूँ।	I am an atheist.

16 English-Hindi Word List

16. English-Hindi Word List

A

able to, to be (V.I.)	***pānā/saknā***	पाना/सकना
about x (PP)	***x ke bāre mẽ***	x के बारे में
above (ADV)	***ūpar***	ऊपर
above x (PP)	***x ke ūpar***	x के ऊपर
accelerator (M)	***ekselareṭar***	एक्सेलरेटर
accident (F)	***durghaṭnā***	दुर्घटना
address, whereabouts (M)	***patā***	पता
adjoining (ADJ)	***agal-bagal vālā***	अगल-बगल वाला
after x (PP)	***x ke bād***	x के बाद
afternoon (F)	***dopahar***	दोपहर
afterwards (ADV)	***bād mẽ***	बाद में
again (ADV)	***phir***	फिर
age (F)	***umr***	उम्र
ago (ADV)	***pehle***	पहले
ahead (ADV)	***āge***	आगे
ahead of x (PP)	***x ke āge***	x के आगे
air mail (F)	***havāī ḍāk***	हवाई डाक
airport (M)	***havāī aḍḍā***	हवाई अड्डा
alcohol/wine (F)	***śarāb***	शराब
allergy (F)	***elarjī***	एलर्जी
alone (ADJ)	***akelā***	अकेला
ambulance (M/F)	***embulens***	एम्बुलेंस
another (ADJ)	***dūsrā***	दूसरा
answer; north (M)	***uttar***	उत्तर
answer, to (to give an answer) (V.T.)	***uttar denā***	उत्तर देना
antibiotics (M)	***eṇṭībāyoṭik***	एंटीबायोटिक
any (PRO, ADJ)	***koī***	कोई
April (M)	***aprail***	अप्रैल
appear, to (V.I.) (to be visible)	***dikhnā***	दिखना
appointment (M)	***apāiṇṭmeṇṭ***	अपॉइंटमेंट
area code (M)	***koḍ***	कोड
around x (PP)	***x ke āspās***	x के आसपास
arrival (M)	***āgaman***	आगमन
arrive, to (V.I.)	***pahũcnā***	पहुँचना
ask, to (V.T.)	***pūchnā***	पूछना

asthma (M)	***damā***	दमा
atheist (ADJ, M)	***nāstik***	नास्तिक
ATM (M)	***e. ṭī. em.***	ए० टी० एम०
attach, to (V.I.)	***lagnā***	लगना
attach (V.T.)	***lagānā***	लगाना
attention/meditation (M)	***dhyān***	ध्यान
attention, to give/pay (V.T.)	***dhyān denā***	ध्यान देना
August (M)	***agast***	अगस्त
auspicious (ADJ)	***śubh***	शुभ
auto(rickshaw) (M)	***āṭo***	ऑटो
available, to be (V.I.)	***milnā***	मिलना

B

bad (ADJ)	***<u>kh</u>arāb***	ख़राब
bad (ADJ)	***burā***	बुरा
bag (F)	***thailī***	थैली
bank (M)	***baink***	बैंक
barber (M)	***nāī***	नाई
barfi (a sweet) (F)	***barfī***	बर्फ़ी
battery (M)	***sel***	सेल
battery (F) (car)	***baiṭrī***	बैट्री
beard (F)	***dāṛhī***	दाढ़ी
beautiful (pleasing) (ADJ)	***suhāvnā***	सुहावना
beautiful/handsome (ADJ)	***sundar***	सुंदर
beauty salon (M)	***sailān***	सैलॉन
become, to (V.I.) (to be made)	***bannā***	बनना
become, to (V.I.)	***honā***	होना
bed (F) (cot) (M)	***cārpāī;*** ***palang***	चारपाई; पलंग
beef (M)	***gāy kā gośt***	गाय का गोश्त
beer (F)	***biyar***	बियर
before (ADV)	***pehle***	पहले
before x (PP)	***x ke pehle***	x के पहले
beginning (M)	***śurū***	शुरू
behind (ADV)	***pīche***	पीछे
behind x (PP)	***x ke pīche***	x के पीछे
belief (M)	***yaqīn***	यक़ीन
believe, to (belief to be) (V.I.)	***yaqīn honā***	यक़ीन होना
below (ADV)	***nīce***	नीचे
below x (PP)	***x ke nīce***	x के नीचे

bend (M)	*moṛ*	मोड़
berth (M)	*barth*	बर्थ
best wishes (F, PL)	*śubhkāmnāẽ*	शुभकामनाएँ
bhatura (bread baked on a griddle and deep fried) (M)	*bhaṭūrā*	भटूरा
big (ADJ)	*baṛā*	बड़ा
bill (check) (M)	*bil*	बिल
biriyani (F)	*biryānī*	बिरयानी
birth (M)	*janm*	जन्म
birthday (M)	*janmdin*	जन्मदिन
bite, to (V.T.)	*kāṭnā*	काटना
bitter (ADJ)	*kaṛvā*	कड़वा
black (ADJ)	*kālā*	काला
blanket (M)	*kambal*	कम्बल
blood (M)	*khūn*	ख़ून
blue (ADJ)	*nīlā*	नीला
boat (F)	*nāv*	नाव
boil, to (V.T.)	*ubālnā*	उबालना
boiled (ADJ)	*ublā huā*	उबला हुआ
bother, to (V.T)	*tang karnā*	तंग करना
book (F)	*kitāb*	किताब
book, to (V.T.)	*būking karānā*	बुकिंग कराना
booking (F)	*būking*	बुकिंग
booking office (M)	*būking āfis*	बुकिंग ऑफ़िस
bookstore (F)	*kitāb kī dukān*	किताब की दुकान
bottom (ADV) (below)	*nīce*	नीचे
boy (M)	*laṛkā*	लड़का
bread (roti) (F)	*roṭī/capātī*	रोटी/चपाती
break (M) (car)	*brek*	ब्रेक
break, to (V.I.)	*ṭūṭnā*	टूटना
break down, to (V.I.)	*kharāb honā*	ख़राब होना
breaker (ADJ)	*avarodhak*	अवरोधक
breakfast (M)	*nāśtā*	नाश्ता
breathe, to (V.T.)	*sā̃s lenā*	साँस लेना
breeze (F)	*bayār*	बयार
bridge (M)	*pul*	पुल
bring, to (V.I.)	*lānā*	लाना
brochure (M)	*brośar*	ब्रोशर
brother (M)	*bhāī*	भाई

brown (ADJ)	***bhūrā***	भूरा
Buddhism (M)	***bauddh dharm***	बौद्ध धर्म
Buddhist (ADJ, M)	***bauddh***	बौद्ध
burn, to (V.I.)	***jalnā***	जलना
bus (F)	***bas***	बस
businessman/person (M/F)	***vyāpārī***	व्यापारी
bus terminus (M)	***bas kā aḍḍā***	बस का अड्डा
busy (ADJ)	***vyast***	व्यस्त
butter (M)	***makkhan***	मक्खन
buttermilk (F)	***chāch***	छाछ
button (M)	***baṭan***	बटन
buy, to (V.T.)	***kharīdnā***	ख़रीदना
by (PP)	***se***	से

C

cabbage (F)	***band gobhī***	बंद गोभी
calculation (M)	***hisāb***	हिसाब
calculate, to (V.T.)	***hisāb lagānā***	हिसाब लगाना
call, to (x y) (V.T.)	***x ko y kehnā***	x को y कहना
call, to (V.T.) (summon)	***bulānā***	बुलाना
canceled, to have (V.T.)	***kainsal karānā***	कैंसल कराना
car (F)	***kār/gāṛī***	कार/गाड़ी
care, to take (V.T.)	***khyāl rakhnā***	ख़्याल रखना
carrot (F)	***gājar***	गाजर
catch, to (V.T.)	***pakaṛnā***	पकड़ना
cauliflower (F)	***phūl gobhī***	फूल गोभी
cell phone (M)	***mobāil fon***	मोबाइल फ़ोन
century (F)	***śatabdī***	शताब्दी
certainly (IND)	***zarūr!***	ज़रूर
certificate (M)	***pramān patra***	प्रमाण पत्र
chain (F)	***zanjīr***	ज़ंजीर
chair (F)	***kursī***	कुरसी
change, to (V.I./V.T.)	***badalnā***	बदलना
charger (M)	***cārjar***	चार्जर
chat (spicy fast food) (F)	***cāṭ***	चाट
cheap (ADJ)	***sastā***	सस्ता
check out, to (V.T.) (vacate)	***cek āuṭ karnā***	चेक आउट करना
cheese (M) (paneer)	***panīr***	पनीर
chicken (M)	***murgh***	मुर्ग़
chickpeas (M, PL)	***chole***	छोले

children (M, PL)	***bāl bacce***	बाल बच्चे
choose, to (V.T.)	***pasand karnā***	पसंद करना
Christian (ADJ, M)	***īsāī***	ईसाई
Christianity (M)	***īsāī dharm***	ईसाई धर्म
church (M)	***kalīsā/girjā***	कलीसा/गिरजा
chutney (F)	***caṭnī***	चटनी
cinema hall (M)	***sinemāhāl***	सिनेमाहाल
city (M)	***śehar***	शहर
class (F) (division)	***śreṇī***	श्रेणी
clean, to (V.T.)	***sāf karnā***	साफ़ करना
clear (ADJ)	***sāf***	साफ़
close (ADJ, ADV)	***nazdīk/pās***	नज़दीक/पास
closed (ADJ)	***band***	बंद
closed, to be (ADJ)	***band honā***	बंद होना
cloth (M)	***kapṛā***	कपड़ा
clothes (M, PL)	***kapṛe***	कपड़े
cloth shop (F)	***kapṛe kī dukān***	कपड़े की दुकान
cloud (M)	***bādal***	बादल
clutch (M) (car)	***klac***	क्लच
coat (M)	***koṭ***	कोट
cobbler (M)	***mocī***	मोची
coffee (F)	***kāfī***	कॉफ़ी
cold (F)	***ṭhaṇḍ***	ठंड
cold (ADJ)	***ṭhaṇḍā***	ठंडा
cold (M) (illness)	***zukām***	ज़ुकाम
color (M)	***rang***	रंग
color, to (V.T.)	***rang lagānā***	रंग लगाना
come, to (V.I.)	***ānā***	आना
company (F)	***kampanī***	कम्पनी
computer (M)	***kampyūṭar***	कम्प्यूटर
concern (F)	***cintā***	चिंता
concern/care (F)	***parvāh***	परवाह
confirm, to (V.T.)	***kanfarm karnā***	कन्फ़र्म करना
Congratulations! (IND)	***badhāī ho!/ mubārak ho!***	बधाई हो!/ मुबारक हो!
connection (M)	***kanekśan***	कनेक्शन
contagious (ADJ)	***sankrāmak***	संक्रामक
contract (M)	***anubandh***	अनुबंध
cook, to (food) (V.T.)	***(khānā) pakānā***	(खाना) पकाना

copy (F)	***kāpī***	कॉपी
corner (M)	***konā***	कोना
cotton (F)/cotton (ADJ)	***ruī/sūtī***	रुई/सूती
cotton (home-spun) (F)	***khādī***	खादी
country (M)	***deś***	देश
course (M)	***kors***	कोर्स
credit card (M)	***kreḍiṭ kārḍ***	क्रेडिट कार्ड
cut, to (V.T.)	***kāṭnā***	काटना

D

daily (ADV)	***roz***	रोज़
dal (lentil dish) (F)	***dāl***	दाल
danger (M)	***khatrā***	ख़तरा
dark color (M)	***gehrā rang***	गहरा रंग
date (F)	***tārīkh***	तारीख़
day (M)	***din***	दिन
day after tomorrow (M)	***parsõ***	परसों
day before yesterday (M)	***parsõ***	परसों
daughter (F)	***beṭī***	बेटी
December (M)	***disambar***	दिसंबर
deep (ADJ)	***gehrā***	गहरा
degree (F)	***upādhi***	उपाधि
delay (F)	***der***	देर
delicious (tasty) (ADJ)	***lazīz/svādiṣṭ***	लज़ीज़/स्वादिष्ट
depart(ed) (ADJ)	***ravānā***	रवाना
depart, to (V.I.)	***ravānā honā***	रवाना होना
departure (M)	***prasthān***	प्रस्थान
deposit (M)	***ḍipāziṭ***	डिपॉज़िट
descend, to (alight, get down) (V.I.)	***utarnā***	उतरना
dew (F)	***os/śabnam***	ओस/शबनम
diabetes (M)	***madhumeh***	मधुमेह
dial, to (V.T.) (a number)	***(nambar) milānā***	(नम्बर) मिलाना
diet, to (V.T.)	***ḍāiṭing karnā***	डाइटिंग करना
dining hall (M)	***ḍāining hāl***	डाइनिंग हॉल
dinner (M)	***rāt kā khānā***	रात का खाना
dirt-absorbing (ADJ)	***mailkhor***	मैलख़ोर
disappear, to (V.I.)	***ghāyab honā***	ग़ायब होना
disappeared (ADJ)	***ghāyab***	ग़ायब
discount (F)	***chūṭ/riyāyat***	छूट/रियायत

disease (M)	***rog***	रोग
dissolve, to (V.T.)	***gholnā***	घोलना
divorced (ADJ)	***talāqśudā***	तलाक़शुदा
dizzy, to become (V.I.)	***cakkar ānā***	चक्कर आना
do, to (V.T.)	***karnā***	करना
doctor (M)	***ḍākṭar***	डॉक्टर
dog (M)	***kuttā***	कुत्ता
domestic (flight) (ADJ)	***antardeśīya***	अंतर्देशीय
don't (IND)	***na, mat***	न/मत
door (M)	***darvāzā***	दरवाज़ा
double (room) (ADJ)	***ḍabal***	डबल
download (M)	***ḍāūnloḍ***	डाउनलोड
dress (F)	***ḍres***	ड्रेस
drink, to (V.T.)	***pīnā***	पीना
drive, to (V.T.); to make move	***calānā***	चलाना
drive fast, to (V.T.)	***tez calānā***	तेज़ चलाना
driver (M)	***ḍrāivar***	ड्राइवर
drop (F)	***bū̃d***	बूँद
durable (ADJ)	***ṭikāū***	टिकाऊ

E

early (F, ADV)	***jaldī***	जल्दी
east (M)	***pūrv***	पूर्व
eastern (ADJ)	***pūrvī***	पूर्वी
easy (ADJ)	***āsān***	आसान
eat, to (V.T.)	***khānā***	खाना
eggplant (M)	***baĩgan***	बैंगन
electronic shop (F)	***bijlī kī dukān***	बिजली की दुकान
embassy (M)	***dūtāvas***	दूतावास
email (F)	***ī-mel***	ई-मेल
emergency (M)	***āpatkāl***	आपत्काल
engine (M)	***injan***	इंजन
English (F)	***angrezī***	अंग्रेज़ी
enjoyable (ADJ)	***mazedār***	मज़ेदार
enjoyment, to come (V.I.)	***mazā ānā***	मज़ा आना
enough (ADJ)	***kāfī***	काफ़ी
Enough! (VOC)	***bas!***	बस!
entire (ADJ)	***pūrā***	पूरा
evening (F)	***śām***	शाम
excellent (ADJ)	***baṛhiyā***	बढ़िया

expensive (ADJ)	*mahẽgā*	महँगा
experience (M)	*anubhav*	अनुभव
exportation (M)	*niryāt*	निर्यात
express post (M)	*ekspres posṭ*	एक्स्प्रेस पोस्ट
express train (F)	*ekspres gāṛī*	एक्स्प्रेस गाड़ी
extra (ADJ, ADV) (more)	*zyādā*	ज़्यादा
eye (F)	*ā̃kh*	आँख
F		
factory (F)	*faikṭrī*	फ़ैक्टरी
fair (ADJ)	*gorā*	गोरा
fake (ADJ)	*naqlī*	नक़ली
fall, to (V.I.)	*girnā*	गिरना
family (M)	*parivār*	परिवार
far (ADJ, ADV)	*dūr*	दूर
fast (for Hindus) (M)	*vrat*	व्रत
fast (for Muslims) (M)	*rozā*	रोज़ा
February (F)	*farvarī*	फ़रवरी
feel (x), to (V.I.)	*(x kā) ehsās honā*	(x का) एहसास होना
fever (M)	*bu<u>kh</u>ār*	बुख़ार
fill, to (V.I./V.T.)	*bharnā*	भरना
film (F)	*film*	फ़िल्म
filtered (ADJ)	*filṭarḍ*	फ़िल्टर्ड
final (ADJ)	*ā<u>kh</u>irī*	आख़िरी
fine (ADJ)	*ṭhīk*	ठीक
fine (penalty) (M)	*jurmānā*	जुर्माना
finished, to be (V.I.)	*<u>kh</u>atm honā*	ख़त्म होना
fire (F)	*āg*	आग
fire extinguisher (M)	*āg bujhāne kā sādhan*	आग बुझाने का साधन
first (ADJ)	*pehlā;* *pratham*	पहला; प्रथम
fish (F)	*machlī*	मछली
fish shop (F)	*machlī kī dukān*	मछली की दुकान
flash (F)	*flaiś*	फ़्लैश
flight (F)	*flāiṭ*	फ़्लाइट
flu (M)	*flū*	फ़्लू
flyover (M)	*flāī-ovar*	फ़्लाइ-ओवर
fog (M)	*kuhrā*	कुहरा
food (M)	*khānā*	खाना

for (the sake of) x (PP)	***x ke liye***	x के लिये
forbidden (ADJ)	***niṣedh/manā***	निषेध/मना
foreign tourist quota (M)	***ṭūrisṭ koṭā***	टूरिस्ट कोटा
forget, to (V.I.)	***bhūlnā***	भूलना
forgive, to (V.T.)	***māf karnā***	माफ़ करना
fort (M)	***qilā***	क़िला
fresh (ADJ)	***tāzā***	ताज़ा
Friday (M)	***śukra(vār)***	शुक्र(वार)
friend (M/F)	***dost***	दोस्त
from (PP)	***se***	से
from there (ADV)	***vahā̃ se***	वहाँ से
fruit (M)	***phal***	फल
G		
game (M)	***khel***	खेल
garage (M)	***gairāj***	गैराज
garden (M)	***ba<u>gh</u>īcā***	बग़ीचा
garlic (M)	***lehsun***	लहसुन
gear (M)	***giyar***	गियर
genuine (ADJ)	***aslī***	असली
get/obtain, to (to be obtained) (V.I.)	***milnā***	मिलना
get down, to (alight, descend) (V.I.)	***utarnā***	उतरना
ghee (M)	***ghī***	घी
girl (F)	***laṛkī***	लड़की
give, to (V.T.)	***denā***	देना
glasses (M)	***caśmā***	चश्मा
go, to (V.I.)	***jānā***	जाना
goat's meat (M)	***bakre kā gośt***	बकरे का गोश्त
God (for Hindus) (M)	***īśvar/bhagvān***	ईश्वर/भगवान
God (for Muslims) (M)	***allāh/<u>kh</u>udā***	अल्लाह/ख़ुदा
God (for Christians) (M)	***prabhu/īśvar***	प्रभु/ईश्वर
God (for Sikhs) (M)	***rab***	रब
good (ADJ)	***acchā***	अच्छा
Goodbye (M)	***namaste/namskār***	नमस्ते/नमस्कार
Good luck (F, PL)	***śubhkāmnāẽ***	शुभकामनाएँ
good morning (M)	***suprabhāt***	सुप्रभात
good night (F)	***śubh rātri***	शुभ रात्रि
goods (M)	***sāmān***	सामान
gourd (F)	***laukī***	लौकी
grateful (ADJ)	***ehsāṇmand***	एहसानमंद

graveyard (M)	***qabristān***	क़ब्रिस्तान
gray (ADJ)	***sleṭī***	स्लेटी
green (ADJ)	***harā***	हरा
grocery (provision) (M)	***parcūn***	परचून
guide (M)	***gāiḍ***	गाइड
gulab jamun (fried sweet made from milk, served hot in syrup) (M)	***gulāb jāmun***	गुलाब जामुन
gurudwara (Sikh temple) (M)	***gurudvāra***	गुरुद्वारा
H		
hail (stone) (M)	***olā***	ओला
hair (M)	***bāl***	बाल
half (ADJ)	***ādhā***	आधा
halva (M)	***halvā***	हलवा
hand (M)	***hāth***	हाथ
handkerchief (M)	***rūmāl***	रूमाल
handsome/beautiful (ADJ)	***sundar***	सुंदर
happen, to (V.I.)	***honā***	होना
happiness (F)	***<u>kh</u>uśī***	ख़ुशी
happy (ADJ)	***<u>kh</u>uś***	ख़ुश
harsh (sharp) (ADJ)	***tez***	तेज़
headache (M)	***sardard***	सरदर्द
health (F) (disposition)	***tabiyat***	तबियत
heart attack (M)	***dil kā daurā***	दिल का दौरा
heart condition (F)	***dil kī bīmārī***	दिल की बीमारी
heat (F)	***garmī***	गर्मी
heavy rain (F)	***mūslādhār bāriś***	मूसलाधार बारिश
hello/goodbye (M)	***namaste***	नमस्ते
hello/goodbye (M)	***namaskār***	नमस्कार
help, to do x's (V.T.)	***x kī madad karnā***	x की मदद करना
here (ADV)	***yahā̃***	यहाँ
high (harsh) wind (F)	***tez havā***	तेज़ हवा
Hindu (ADJ, M)	***hindū***	हिन्दू
Hinduism (M)	***hindū dharm***	हिंदू धर्म
historical (ADJ)	***aitihāsik***	ऐतिहासिक
hither (ADV)	***idhar***	इधर
hobby (M)	***śauq***	शौक़
hold, to (V.T.) (to wait on the line)	***holḍ karnā***	होल्ड करना
home (M)	***ghar***	घर
hope (F)	***ummīd***	उम्मीद

hospital (M)	***aspatāl***	अस्पताल
hot (ADJ)	***garm***	गर्म
hot wind (F)	***lū***	लू
hour; bell (M)	***ghaṇṭā***	घंटा
how (ADJ)	***kaisā***	कैसा
how much/many (ADJ)	***kitnā***	कितना
humidity (F)	***umas***	उमस
hundred (M)	***sau***	सौ
hunger (F)	***bhūkh***	भूख
hungry, to feel (to x) (V.I.)	***(x ko) bhūkh lagnā***	(x को) भूख लगना
husband (M)	***pati***	पति
I		
ice (F)	***barf***	बर्फ़
icy wind (F)	***barfīlī hava***	बर्फ़ीली हवा
I.D. card (M)	***āī. ḍī. kārḍ***	आई० डी० कार्ड
ill (ADJ)	***bīmār***	बीमार
immigration (M)	***apravāsan***	अप्रवासन
important (ADJ)	***aham***	अहम
importation (M)	***āyāt***	आयात
in (PP)	***mẽ***	में
incline (F)	***ḍhalān***	ढलान
included (ADJ)	***śāmil***	शामिल
India (M)	***bhārat***	भारत
infection (M)	***infekśan***	इन्फ़ेक्शन
in fine fettle (ADV)	***maze mẽ***	मज़े में
information (F)	***jānkārī***	जानकारी
injection (F)	***suī***	सुई
injury (F)	***coṭ***	चोट
injured, to become (V.I.) (x)	***(x ko) coṭ lagnā***	(x को) चोट लगना
inside (ADV)	***andar***	अंदर
inside x (ADV)	***x ke andar***	x के अंदर
install (V.T.)	***insṭāl karnā***	इनस्टाल करना
international (ADJ)	***antarrāṣṭrīya***	अंतर्राष्ट्रीय
Internet (M)	***inṭarneṭ/indrajāl***	इंटरनेट/इंद्रजाल
Internet café (M)	***inṭarneṭ kaife***	इंटरनेट कैफ़े
intersection (M)	***caurāhā***	चौराहा
in the middle (ADV)	***bīc mẽ***	बीच में
issue (matter) (M)	***māmlā***	मामला
issue, to (V.T.)	***jārī karnā***	जारी करना

insurance (M)	***bīmā***	बीमा
interpreter (English speaker) (M)	***angrezī bolnevālā***	अंग्रेज़ी बोलनेवाला
Islam (M)	***islām***	इसलाम
J		
Jain (ADJ, M)	***jain***	जैन
jalebi (fried crisp sweet in syrup) (F)	***jalebī***	जलेबी
January (F)	***janvarī***	जनवरी
jewelry shop (F)	***zevrāt kī dukān***	ज़ेवरात की दुकान
Jewish (ADJ, M)	***yahūdī***	यहूदी
job (F)	***naukrī***	नौकरी
job, to do a (for money) (V.T.)	***naukrī karnā***	नौकरी करना
journey (F)	***yātrā***	यात्रा
Judaism (M)	***yahūdī dharm***	यहूदी धर्म
juice (M)	***ras/jūs***	रस/जूस
July (F)	***julāī***	जुलाई
June (M)	***jūn***	जून
K		
keep, to (place) (V.T.)	***rakhnā***	रखना
key (F)	***cābī***	चाबी
khoya (solidified milk) (M)	***khoyā***	खोया
kidney beans (M, PL)	***rājmā***	राजमा
know, to (to come to x) (V.I.)	***(x ko) ānā***	(x को) आना
know, to (to be known to x) (V.I.)	***(x ko) mālūm honā***	(x को) मालूम होना
know, to (V.T.)	***jānnā***	जानना
kulfi (F)	***qulfī***	कुलफ़ी
L		
laddu (sweet made from chickpea flour) (M)	***laḍḍū***	लड्डू
laneway (F)	***galī***	गली
laptop (M)	***lepṭāp***	लैपटॉप
lassi (F)	***lassī***	लस्सी
late (ADV)	***der se***	देर से
late, to be (V.I.) (lateness to happen)	***der honā***	देर होना
later (afterwards) (ADV)	***bād mẽ***	बाद में
lawyer (M)	***vakīl***	वकील
leather (M)/leather (ADJ)	***camṛā/camṛe kā***	चमड़ा/चमड़े का
leave, to (abandon) (V.T.)	***choṛnā***	छोड़ना
left side (ADV)	***bāyī̃ tarf/or***	बायीं तरफ़/ओर
lentils (F)	***dāl***	दाल

English-Hindi Word List

16

letter (M)	***patra;***	पत्र;
(F)	***ciṭṭhī***	चिट्ठी
license (M)	***lāisens***	लाइसेंस
lie down, to (V.I.)	***leṭnā***	लेटना
light (F)	***battī***	बत्ती
light color (M)	***halkā rang***	हल्का रंग
light rain (F)	***bū̃dābā̃dī***	बूँदाबाँदी
like, to (to be liked, preferred) to x (V.I.)	***x ko pasand honā***	x को पसंद होना
like, to (to seem good) to x (V.I.)	***x ko acchā lagnā***	अच्छा लगना
limit (F)	***sīmā***	सीमा
line (F)	***lāin***	लाइन
listen, to (V.T.)	***sunnā***	सुनना
little (ADJ)	***thoṛā***	थोड़ा
live, to (V.I.)	***rehnā***	रहना
long (ADJ)	***lambā***	लम्बा
lose, to (V.T.) (an item)	***khonā***	खोना
lost, to become (V.I.)	***khonā***	खोना
love (M)	***pyār***	प्यार
love, to (V.T.)	***pyār karnā***	प्यार करना
low beam (M) (car)	***ḍipar***	डिपर
luggage (M)	***sāmān***	सामान
lunch (M)	***din kā khānā***	दिन का खाना
M		
machine (F)	***maśīn***	मशीन
make, to (V.T.)	***banānā***	बनाना
man (M)	***ādmī***	आदमी
manager (M)	***prabandhak***	प्रबंधक
map (M)	***naqśā***	नक़्शा
March (M)	***mārc***	मार्च
market (M)	***bāzār***	बाज़ार
married (ADJ)	***śādīśudā, vivāhit***	शादीशुदा, विवाहित
massage (F)	***māliś***	मालिश
massage, to (V.T.)	***māliś karnā***	मालिश करना
match (M)	***maic***	मैच
matter (F)	***bāt***	बात
mausoleum (M)	***maqbarā***	मक़बरा
May (F)	***maī***	मई
meaning (M)	***matlab***	मतलब

meanwhile (ADV)	***bīc mẽ***	बीच में
meat (M)	***māns/gośt***	मांस/गोश्त
medication (F)	***davā***	दवा
medicine (F)	***davā***	दवा
meet, to (V.I.)	***milnā***	मिलना
member (M)	***membar***	मेम्बर
memory card (M)	***memrī kārḍ***	मेमरी कार्ड
mend, to (V.T.)	***x kī marammat karnā***	x की मरम्मत करना
menstruation (M)	***māsik dharm***	मासिकधर्म
menu (M)	***menū kārḍ***	मेनू कार्ड
meter (M)	***mīṭar***	मीटर
metro (F)	***meṭro***	मेट्रो
metro station (M)	***meṭro sṭeśan***	मेट्रो स्टेशन
midday (F)	***dopahar***	दोपहर
middle (ADV)	***bīc***	बीच
mind; heart (M)	***man***	मन
minute (M)	***minaṭ***	मिनट
mirror (M)	***āinā***	आइना
miss, to (the memory to come to) (V.I.)	***yād ānā***	याद आना
mixed (ADJ)	***milā-julā***	मिला-जुला
mobile phone (M)	***mobāil fon***	मोबाइल फ़ोन
mobile phone shop (F)	***mobāil fon kī dukān***	मोबाइल फ़ोन की दुकान
Monday (M)	***somvār***	सोमवार
money order (M)	***manī ārḍar***	मनी ऑर्डर
monkey (M)	***bandar***	बंदर
month (M)	***mahīnā***	महीना
morning (M) (F)	***saverā;*** ***subah***	सवेरा; सुबह
mosque (F)	***masjid***	मस्जिद
mosquito (M)	***macchar***	मच्छर
mosquito net (F)	***macchardānī***	मच्छरदानी
moustache (F)	***mũ̃ch***	मूँछ
mouth (M)	***mũh***	मुँह
move, to (V.I.)	***calnā***	चलना
movie (F)	***film***	फ़िल्म
muffler (M)	***maflar***	मफ़लर
multinational corporation (F)	***bahurāṣṭrīya kampanī***	बहुराष्ट्रीय कम्पनी

English-Hindi Word List 16

muscle (F)	***mānspeśī***	मांसपेशी
museum (M)	***sangrahālay/myuziyam***	संग्रहालय/म्यूज़ियम
music (M)	***sangīt***	संगीत
Muslim (ADJ, M)	***musalmān/muslim***	मुसलमान/मुसलिम
mutton (M)	***bheṛ kā gośt***	भेड़ का गोश्त
N		
name (M)	***nām***	नाम
nan (F)	***nān***	नान
nationality (F)	***nāgriktā***	नागरिकता
necessary (ADJ)	***zarūrī***	ज़रूरी
necessity (F)	***zarūrat***	ज़रूरत
new (ADJ)	***nayā***	नया
next (ADJ)	***aglā***	अगला
next to (ADV)	***pās***	पास
nice (good) (ADJ)	***acchā***	अच्छा
night (F)	***rāt***	रात
no (ADV)	***jī nahī̃***	जी नहीं
noise (M) (commotion)	***śorgul***	शोरगुल
noise (F) (sound, voice)	***āvāz***	आवाज़
north; answer (M)	***uttar***	उत्तर
not (IND)	***nahī̃***	नहीं
note, to (V.T.)	***noṭ karnā***	नोट करना
nothing (PRON)	***kuch nahī̃***	कुछ नहीं
November (M)	***navambar***	नवम्बर
nowhere (ADV)	***kahī̃ nahī̃***	कहीं नहीं
number (M)	***nambar***	नम्बर
O		
ocean (M)	***samudra***	समुद्र
occupation (M)	***peśā***	पेशा
o'clock (ADV)	***baje***	बजे
October (M)	***aktūbar***	अक्तूबर
office (M)	***daftar***	दफ़्तर
oil (M)	***tel***	तेल
ointment (M)	***marham***	मरहम
old/big (ADJ)	***baṛā***	बड़ा
old (ADJ) (in duration)	***purānā***	पुराना
on (PP)	***par/pe***	पर/पे
one's own (ADJ)	***apnā***	अपना
one-way (ADJ)	***ek-tarafā***	एक-तरफ़ा

onion (M)	***pyāz***	प्याज़
online (ADJ)	***ān-lāin***	ऑन-लाइन
only (ADV+ADJ)	***sirf***	सिर्फ़
on route (ADV) (in the middle)	***bīc mẽ***	बीच में
open (ADJ)	***khulā***	खुला
open, to (V.I.)	***khulnā***	खुलना
open, to (V.T.)	***kholnā***	खोलना
operation (M)	***āpareśan***	आपरेशन
opinion (M) (F)	***khyāl/vicār*** ***rāy***	ख़्याल/विचार राय
optician (optical store) (F)	***caśme kī dukān***	चश्मे की दुकान
orange (ADJ, F)	***nārangī***	नारंगी
orange juice (sweet lime) (M)	***mausamī kā ras***	मौसमी का रस
order, to (to give the order) (V.T.)	***ārḍar denā***	ऑर्डर देना
order, to take (to take the order) (V.T.)	***ārḍar lenā***	ऑर्डर लेना
outside (ADV)	***bāhar***	बाहर
outside x (PP)	***x ke bāhar***	x के बाहर
over here (ADV)	***idhar***	इधर
over there (ADV)	***udhar***	उधर
owner (M)	***mālik***	मालिक

P

pain (M)	***dard***	दर्द
paisa (M)	***paisā***	पैसा
pants (F)	***paĩṭ***	पैंट
paratha (M) (fried bread, unleaved wheat flour)	***parā̃ṭhā***	पराँठा
parcel (M)	***pārsal***	पार्सल
parents (M, PL)	***mātā-pitā***	माता-पिता
park (M)	***pārk***	पार्क
park, to (V.T.)	***gāṛī lagānā***	गाड़ी लगाना
partner (M)	***sāthī***	साथी
passport (M)	***pārpatra***	पारपत्र
path (M)	***rāstā***	रास्ता
pay, to (V.T.)	***bhugtān karnā***	भुगतान करना
pay the bill, to (V.T.)	***bil cukānā***	बिल चुकाना
pea (F)	***maṭar***	मटर
pedal (M) (car/bike)	***paiḍal***	पैडल
perhaps (IND)	***śāyad***	शायद
permission, to give (V.T.)	***ijāzat denā***	इजाज़त देना

permit (M)	*parmiṭ*	परमिट
person (man) (M)	*ādmī*	आदमी
petrol (M)	*peṭrol; tel*	पेट्रोल; तेल
pharmacy (M)	*davākhānā*	दवाख़ाना
phone, to (V.T.)	*fon karnā*	फ़ोन करना
phone card (M)	*fon kārḍ*	फ़ोन कार्ड
photo (F) (M/F)	*tasvīr;* *foṭo*	तस्वीर; फ़ोटो
pickle (M)	*acār*	अचार
pick up, to (V.T.)	*uṭhānā*	उठाना
piece (M)	*pīs*	पीस
piece (M)	*ṭukṛā*	टुकड़ा
pill (F)	*golī*	गोली
pink (ADJ)	*gulābī*	गुलाबी
place (M) (F)	*sthān;* *jagah*	स्थान; जगह
play, to (V.I./V.T.)	*khelnā*	खेलना
pneumonia (M)	*nimoniyā*	निमोनिया
police (F)	*pulis*	पुलिस
police station (M)	*thānā*	थाना
polish, to (V.T.)	*camkānā*	चमकाना
pollution (M)	*pradūṣaṇ*	प्रदूषण
pool (M)	*pūl*	पूल
pond (M)	*tālāb*	तालाब
porter (M)	*porṭar*	पोर्टर
postcard (M)	*posṭkārḍ*	पोस्टकार्ड
post office (M)	*ḍākkhānā*	डाकख़ाना
potato (M)	*ālū*	आलू
prayer (for Hindus) (F)	*prārthnā*	प्रार्थना
prayer (for Christians) (F)	*prārthnā*	प्रार्थना
prayer (formal) (for Muslims) (F)	*namāz*	नमाज़
prayer (for Muslims) (F)	*duā*	दुआ
preferred (ADJ)	*pasand*	पसंद
pregnant (ADJ)	*garbhvatī*	गर्भवती
prescription (M)	*nuskhā*	नुस्ख़ा
pressure (M)	*preśar*	प्रेशर
previous (ADJ)	*pichlā*	पिछला
previously (ADV)	*pehle*	पहले
price (M)	*dām*	दाम

printer (M)	***priṇṭar***	प्रिंटर
profession (M)	***peśā***	पेशा
professional (ADJ)	***peśevar***	पेशेवर
properly (ADV)	***ṭhīk se***	ठीक से
provision (grocery) (M)	***parcūn***	परचून
public (ADJ)	***sārvajanik***	सार्वजनिक
pumpkin (M)	***kaddū***	कद्दू
pure (ADJ)	***śudh***	शुद्ध
puri (fried bread) (F)	***pūṛī***	पूड़ी
purple (ADJ)	***baiganī***	बैगनी
purse (M)	***baṭuā***	बटुआ
put/pour, to (V.T.)	***ḍālnā***	डालना
pyjama (M) (type of pant)	***paijāmā***	पैजामा
Q		
qualified (ADJ)	***dakṣ***	दक्ष
quickly (ADV)	***jaldī***	जल्दी
R		
radiator (M) (car)	***reḍiyeṭar***	रेडियेटर
rain (F)	***bāriś***	बारिश
rain, to (V.I.)	***bāriś honā***	बारिश होना
raincoat (F)	***barsātī***	बरसाती
rainy season (M, PL)	***barsāt ke din***	बरसात के दिन
rape (M)	***balātkār***	बलात्कार
rasmalai (sweet dish, made of cream, milk and syrup) (F)	***rasmalāī***	रसमलाई
read/study, to (V.T.)	***paṛhnā***	पढ़ना
ready (ADJ)	***taiyār***	तैयार
real (ADJ)	***aslī***	असली
receipt (F)	***rasīd***	रसीद
red (ADJ)	***lāl***	लाल
reduce, to (V.T.)	***kam karnā***	कम करना
registered post (M)	***registarḍ posṭ***	रेजिस्टर्ड पोस्ट
relate, to, (V.T.)	***sunānā***	सुनाना
religion (for Hinduism and others) (M)	***dharm***	धर्म
religion (for Islam) (M)	***mazhab***	मज़हब
religious (ADJ)	***dhārmik***	धार्मिक
religious site (M)	***dhārmik sthal***	धार्मिक स्थल
remain, to (stay, live) (V.I.)	***rehnā***	रहना

remember, x to (to be remembered to x) (V.I.)	***x ko yād honā***	x को याद होना
rent, to (to take on rent) (V.T.)	***kirāye par lenā***	किराये पर लेना
rental (M)	***kirāyā***	किराया
reservation, to make (have done) (V.T.)	***ārakṣaṇ karānā***	आरक्षण कराना
reserve, to (V.T.)	***ārakṣaṇ karnā***	आरक्षण करना
restaurant (M)	***restrā̃***	रेस्ट्राँ
return, to (V.I.) (come back)	***vāpas ānā***	वापस आना
return, to (V.T.) (something)	***vāpas karnā***	वापस करना
return(ed) (ADJ)	***vāpas***	वापस
return ticket (M/F)	***vāpasī ṭikaṭ***	वापसी टिकट
rice (M)	***cāval***	चावल
rice pudding (F)	***khīr***	खीर
right now (ADV)	***abhī***	अभी
right side (ADV)	***dāhinī taraf/or***	दाहिनी तरफ़/ओर
road (path) (M)	***mārg***	मार्ग
robbery (F)	***corī***	चोरी
robbery, to happen (V.I.)	***corī honā***	चोरी होना
room (M)	***kamrā***	कमरा
roti (bread) (F)	***roṭī***	रोटी
rouse, to (V.T.)	***uṭhānā***	उठाना
rupee (M)	***rupayā***	रुपया
S		
sad (ADJ)	***dukhī***	दुखी
sadness (M)	***dukh***	दुख
safe (for valuables) (F)	***tijorī***	तिजोरी
safely (ADV)	***sahī-salāmat***	सही-सलामत
salary (M)	***vetan***	वेतन
salt (M)	***namak***	नमक
salty (ADJ)	***namkīn***	नमकीन
salwar (type of pant) (F)	***salvār***	सलवार
sambhar (M)	***sā̃bhar***	साँभर
samosa (M)	***samosā***	समोसा
sandals (F)	***cappal***	चप्पल
sari (F)	***sāṛī***	साड़ी
Saturday (M)	***śani(vār)/ śaniścar***	शनिवार/शनिश्चर
savory (ADJ)	***namkīn***	नमकीन
say, to (V.T.)	***kehnā***	कहना

scan, to (V.T.)	***skain karnā***	स्कैन करना
scanner (M)	***skainar***	स्कैनर
scarf (M)	***dupaṭṭā***	दुपट्टा
search, to (V.T.)	***talāś karnā***	तलाश करना
season (M)	***mausam***	मौसम
seat (F)	***sīṭ/ kursī***	सीट/कुरसी
second (other) (ADJ)	***dūsrā***	दूसरा
second time (ADV)	***dubārā***	दुबारा
see/watch, to (V.T.)	***dekhnā***	देखना
seem, to (V.I.)	***lagnā***	लगना
seem right, to (V.I.)	***ṭhīk lagnā***	ठीक लगना
sell, to (V.T.)	***becnā***	बेचना
send, to (V.T.)	***bhejnā***	भेजना
senior (elder) (ADJ)	***buzurg***	बुज़ुर्ग
September (M)	***sitambar***	सितम्बर
serious (ADJ)	***gabhīr***	गंभीर
sex (male/female) (M)	***ling (puruṣ/strī)***	लिंग (पुरुष/स्त्री)
sharp (ADJ)	***tīvra***	तीव्र
shave a beard, to (V.T.)	***dāṛhī banānā***	दाढ़ी बनाना
shave a moustache, to (V.T.)	***mū̃chẽ kāṭnā***	मूँछें काटना
shawl (M)	***śāl***	शॉल
sheet (bed) (F)	***cādar***	चादर
Shia (ADJ, M) (one of the two major sects of Islam)	***śiyā***	शिया
shiny (ADJ)	***camkīlā***	चमकीला
shoe (M)	***jūtā***	जूता
shoe lace (M)	***fītā***	फ़ीता
shop, to (to do shopping) (V.T.)	***śāpiṅg karnā***	शॉपिंग करना
show (M)	***śo***	शो
show, to (V.T.)	***dikhānā***	दिखाना
shirt (F) (M)	***kamīz;*** ***kurtā***	कमीज़; कुरता
sick (ADJ)	***bīmār***	बीमार
side (M) (F)	***kinārā;*** ***taraf***	किनारा; तरफ़
sign (M)	***niśān***	निशान
sign, to (V.T.)	***hastākṣar karnā***	हस्ताक्षर करना
signature (M, PL)	***hastākṣar***	हस्ताक्षर
Sikh (ADJ, M)	***sikkh***	सिक्ख

Sikhism (M)	*sikkh dharm*	सिक्ख धर्म
silk (M)/silk (ADJ)	*reśam/reśmī*	रेशम/रेशमी
sim card (M)	*sim kārḍ*	सिम कार्ड
single (room) (ADJ)	*singal*	सिंगल
Sir (M)	*(bhāī) sāhab*	(भाई) साहब
sister (F)	*behan*	बहन
sit, to (V.I.)	*baiṭhnā*	बैठना
site (M) (place)	*sthān*	स्थान
skin (F)	*khāl*	खाल
sky (M)	*āsmān*	आसमान
sleep, to (V.I.)	*sonā*	सोना
slope (F)	*ḍhalān*	ढलान
slow (ADJ)	*dhīmā*	धीमा
slowly (ADV)	*dhīre*	धीरे
small (ADJ)	*choṭā*	छोटा
smile (F)	*muskān*	मुस्कान
smoking (M)	*dhūmrapān*	धूम्रपान
snack (M)	*namkīn*	नमकीन
snow (F)	*barf*	बर्फ़
soap (M)	*sābun*	साबुन
socks (M, PL)	*moze*	मोज़े
soda (M)	*soḍā*	सोडा
sole (M)	*talā*	तला
some, something (PRON, ADJ)	*kuch*	कुछ
some more (ADJ)	*kuch aur*	कुछ और
somewhere (ADV)	*kahī̃*	कहीं
so much (ADJ)	*itnā*	इतना
son (M)	*beṭā*	बेटा
sorrow (M)	*afsos*	अफ़सोस
sour (ADJ)	*khaṭṭā*	खट्टा
south (M)	*dakṣiṇ*	दक्षिण
spam (M)	*spaim*	स्पैम
speak, to (V.I./V.T.)	*bolnā*	बोलना
speed (F)	*gati*	गति
speed, to (V.T.)	*tez gati se gāṛī calānā*	तेज़ गति से गाड़ी चलाना
spicy (ADJ)	*tīkhā*	तीखा
spinach (M)	*pālak*	पालक
spoon (M)	*cammac*	चम्मच

sports store (F)	*khel-kūd ke sāmān kī dukān*	खेल-कूद के सामान की दुकान
sprain, to come (V.I.)	*moc ānā*	मोच आना
stale (ADJ)	*bāsī*	बासी
stamp (M/F)	*ṭikaṭ*	टिकट
statement (M)	*bayān*	बयान
station (M)	*sṭeśan*	स्टेशन
statue (F)	*mūrti*	मूर्ति
stay, to (V.I.) (remain, live)	*rahnā*	रहना
stay, to (V.I.) (to tarry, stop)	*ṭheharnā*	ठहरना
stay away, to (V.I.)	*dūr rehnā*	दूर रहना
STD (M)	*gupt rog*	गुप्त रोग
steering wheel (M)	*cakkā*	चक्का
stomach (M)	*peṭ*	पेट
stool (F) (faeces)	*ṭaṭṭī*	टट्टी
stop/wait, to (V.I.)	*ruknā*	रुकना
store (F)	*dukān*	दुकान
storm (F)	*ā̃dhī*	आँधी
straight (ADJ)	*sīdhā*	सीधा
straight ahead (ADV)	*sīdhe*	सीधे
street (F)	*saṛak*	सड़क
strike, to (V.I.)	*bajnā*	बजना
stroll, to (V.I.)	*ṭehalnā*	टहलना
stuck, to become (V.I.)	*phā̃snā*	फँसना
student (M)	*chātra*	छात्र
student (F)	*chātrā*	छात्रा
study/read, to (V.T.)	*paṛhnā*	पढ़ना
suit (M)	*sūṭ*	सूट
summer (M, PL)	*garmī ke din*	गर्मी के दिन
Sunday (M)	*ravi(vār)/itvār*	रविवार/इतवार
sunlight (F)	*dhūp*	धूप
Sunni (ADJ, M) (one of the two major sects of Islam)	*sunnī*	सुन्नी
supermarket (M)	*suparmārkeṭ*	सुपरमार्केट
swallow, to (V.T.)	*nigalnā*	निगलना
sweater (M)	*sveṭar*	स्वेटर
sweet (taste) (ADJ)	*mīṭhā*	मीठा
sweet shop (F)	*miṭhāī kī dukān*	मिठाई की दुकान
swim, to (V.I./V.T.)	*tairnā*	तैरना

switch off, to (V.T.)	*band karnā*	बंद करना
synthetic (ADJ)	*banāvaṭī*	बनावटी

T

table (F)	*mez*	मेज़
tablet (F)	*golī*	गोली
tailor (M)	*darzī*	दर्ज़ी
take, to (V.T.)	*lenā*	लेना
take a photo, to (V.T.)	*foṭo/tasvīr khī̃cnā*	फ़ोटो खींचना
take off, to (V.T.)	*utārnā*	उतारना
talk, to (V.T.) (to x)	*(x se) bāt karnā*	(x से) बात करना
tasty (delicious) (ADJ)	*lazīz/svādiṣṭ*	लज़ीज़/स्वादिष्ट
tax (M)	*śulk*	शुल्क
taxi (F)	*ṭaiksī*	टैक्सी
tea (F)	*cāī*	चाय
teacher (M/F)	*ṭīcar*	टीचर
tell, to (V.T.)	*batānā*	बताना
temperature (M)	*tāpmān*	तापमान
temple (M)	*mandir*	मंदिर
testing (F) (examination)	*jā̃c*	जाँच
Thank you (M)	*śukriyā*	शुक्रिया
that (PRON)	*voh*	वह
there (ADV)	*vahā̃*	वहाँ
these (PRON)	*ye*	ये
these days (ADV)	*ājkal*	आजकल
thief (M)	*cor*	चोर
thing (F)	*bāt*	बात
thing (F) (material object)	*cīz*	चीज़
think, to (v.t.)	*socnā*	सोचना
thirst (F)	*pyās*	प्यास
thirsty to feel (to x) (V.I.)	*(x ko) pyās lagnā*	(x को) प्यास लगना
this (PRON)	*yeh*	यह
thither (ADV)	*udhar*	उधर
those (PRON)	*vo*	वे
thousand (M)	*hazār*	हज़ार
Thursday (M)	*guru(vār)/bṛhaspativār*	गुरु(वार)/ बृहस्पतिवार
ticket (M/F)	*ṭikaṭ*	टिकट
time (M)	*samay/ṭāim*	समय/टाइम
timetable (F)	*samay sārṇī*	समय सारणी

English-Hindi Word List 16

tip (F)	***bakhśīś***	बख़्शीश
tire, tyre (M)	***pahiyā***	पहिया
tobacconist (F)	***pān kī dukān***	पान की दुकान
today (ADV)	***āj***	आज
toilet (M)	***śaucālay/ṭāyleṭ***	शौचालय/टॉयलेट
toilet paper (M)	***ṭāyleṭ pepar***	टॉयलेट पेपर
tomorrow (M)	***kal***	कल
tonight (F)	***āj rāt***	आज रात
top (ADV) (above)	***ūpar***	ऊपर
touch, to (V.T.)	***chūnā***	छूना
tour (M)	***ṭūr***	टूर
tourist (M)	***paryaṭak***	पर्यटक
tourist quota (M)	***ṭūrisṭ koṭā***	टूरिस्ट कोटा
town (M)	***nagar***	नगर
traffic light (F)	***battī***	बत्ती
train (F)	***ṭren/relgāṛī/gāṛī***	ट्रेन/रेलगाड़ी/गाड़ी
training (M)	***praśikṣaṇ***	प्रशिक्षण
transfer (M)	***sthānāntaraṇ***	स्थानांतरण
trapped, to become (V.I.)	***phāsnā***	फँसना
travel/wander, to (V.I.)	***ghūmnā***	घूमना
travel, to (V.T.)	***yātrā karnā***	यात्रा करना
traveler (M)	***yātrī***	यात्री
trip (F)	***yātrā***	यात्रा
trunk (F) (car)	***ḍikkī***	डिक्की
t-shirt (F)	***ṭī śarṭ***	टी शर्ट
Tuesday (M)	***maṅgal(vār)***	मंगल(वार)
turn, to (V.I.)	***muṛnā***	मुड़ना
twenty-four hours (ADV)	***caubīs ghaṇṭe***	चौबीस घंटे
Twitter (M)	***ṭviṭar***	ट्विटर
two-way (ADJ)	***do-tarafā***	दो-तरफ़ा
U		
ulcer (M)	***alsar***	अलसर
understand, to (V.T.)	***samajhnā***	समझना
unemployed (ADJ)	***berozgār***	बेरोज़गार
unleaded (petrol) (ADJ)	***anleḍeḍ***	अनलेडेड
unmarried (ADJ)	***avivāhit***	अविवाहित
until, up to (PP)	***tak***	तक
urinate, to (V.T.)	***peśāb karnā***	पेशाब करना

use (x), to (V.T.)	***(x kā) istemāl karnā***	(x का) इस्तेमाल करना

V

vacate, to (V.T.)	***<u>kh</u>ālī karnā***	ख़ाली करना
valuable (ADJ)	***beśqīmtī***	बेशक़ीमती
vegetable (dish) (F)	***sabzī***	सब्ज़ी
vegetarian (ADJ)	***śākāhārī***	शाकाहारी
very (ADJ, ADV)	***bahut***	बहुत
via (ADV)	***x se ho kar***	x से होकर
vigilance (F)	***sāvadhānī***	सावधानी
virus (M)	***vāiras***	वाइरस
visible, to be (V.I.)	***dikhāī denā***	दिखाई देना
vomit, to (V.I.)	***ulṭī honā***	उल्टी होना

W

wait/stop, to (V.I.)	***ruknā***	रुकना
wait, to (for x) (V.T.)	***x kā intazār karnā***	x का इंतज़ार करना
wallet (M)	***baṭuā***	बटुआ
want to, to (V.T.)	***cāhnā***	चाहना
want/need (an object) (V.I.)	***cāhiye***	चाहिये
wash, to (V.T.)	***dhonā***	धोना
water (M)	***pānī***	पानी
way (M) (path)	***rāstā***	रास्ता
wear, to (V.T.)	***pehannā***	पहनना
weather (M)	***mausam***	मौसम
web browser (M)	***veb brāuzar***	वेब ब्राउज़र
wedding (F)	***śādī***	शादी
Wednesday (M)	***budh(vār)***	बुध(वार)
week (M)	***haftā***	हफ़्ता
Well done! (IND)	***śābāś!***	शाबाश!
west (M)	***paścim***	पश्चिम
western (ADJ)	***paścimī***	पश्चिमी
what (PRON)	***kyā***	क्या
when (ADV)	***kab***	कब
where (ADV)	***kahā̃***	कहाँ
which (ADJ)	***kaun-sā***	कौन-सा
whiskey (F)	***whiskī***	ह्विस्की
white (ADJ)	***safed***	सफ़ेद
who (PRON)	***kaun***	कौन

why (ADV)	*kyõ*	क्यों
widow (F)	*vidhvā*	विधवा
widower (M)	*vidhur*	विधुर
wife (F)	*patnī*	पत्नी
wind (F)	*havā*	हवा
window (F)	*khiṛkī*	खिड़की
windshield (glass) (M)	*śīśā*	शीशा
winter (M, PL)	*ṭhaṇḍ ke din*	ठंड के दिन
with (through) (PP)	*se*	से
with (PP)	*x ke sāth*	x के साथ
witness (M)	*gavāh*	गवाह
woman (F)	*aurat*	औरत
wood (F)/wooden (ADJ)	*lakṛī/lakṛī kā*	लकड़ी/लकड़ी का
wool (M)/woollen (ADJ)	*ūn/ūnī*	ऊन/ऊनी
work, to (do) (V.T.)	*kām karnā*	काम करना
worried (ADJ)	*fikramand*	फ़िक्रमंद
worth (ADJ)	*lāyaq*	लायक़
wrap, to (V.T.)	*lapeṭnā*	लपेटना
write, to (V.T.)	*likhnā*	लिखना
wrong (ADJ)	*ghalat*	ग़लत
Y		
year (M)	*sāl*	साल
yellow (ADJ)	*pīlā*	पीला
yes (ADV)	*jī hā̃*	जी हाँ
yesterday (M)	*kal*	कल
yoghurt (M)	*dahī*	दही
young/small (ADJ)	*choṭā*	छोटा
you (PRON, POLITE)	*āp*	आप
you (PRON, INFORMAL)	*tum*	तुम
Z		
zero (ADJ, M)	*śūnya*	शून्य